THE LOST ART OF
LADY HOOD

Published by Familius LLC, www.familius.com

Familius books are available at special discounts for bulk
purchases for sales promotions, family or corporate use. Special
editions, including personalized covers, excerpts of existing books,
or books with corporate logos, can be created in large quantities
for special needs. For more information, contact Premium Sales at
801-552-7298 or email specialmarkets@familius.com.

Library of Congress Catalog-in-Publication Data
2014952332
pISBN 978-1-939629-39-5
eISBN 978-1-939629-99-9

Printed in the United States of America

Edited by Michele Robbins
Book and cover design by David Miles

10 9 8 7 6 5 4 3 2 1

First Edition

THE LOST ART OF LADYHOOD

12 ESSENTIAL SKILLS TO BE CONFIDENT AND CLASSY IN A CRAZY WORLD

JESSIE FUNK

FAMILIUS

✨ DEDICATION

Thank you to all of my "Ivy Girls." (You know who you are.) Each one of your sweet faces motivated me as I struggled in writing this book. Thank you for teaching me and giving me such a strong sense of purpose.

My sweet children, all of my work is for you. Mama loves you.

My darling husband, your support means so much to me. I love you.

Michele, thank you for your patience and taking the time to teach me how to write a book. ("Please let me keep the smiley faces . . . " Haha.)

Lastly, I would like to dedicate this book to a woman I consider to be the ideal "Lady"—my grandmother, Florence Clark. You perfectly exemplified what true loveliness looks and acts like. I hope I can pass on your legacy. I miss you.

CONTENTS

INTRODUCTION

WHY SHOULD I READ THIS BOOK?

Listen, Jessie, I'm a busy teenager with a schedule to keep. Will you be wasting my time with endless talk of doilies? Crossing my ankles? Sitting up straight? Batting my eyelashes while sipping my tea with pinky extended? Is this what it means to be a lady?

Nope! Not unless you live in the early 1800s and enjoy suffocation by corset! Being a lady simply means being confident, being classy, and having solid character. In the world we live in, those three traits need to be reclaimed.

WHY SHOULD I LISTEN TO YOU, JESSIE? WHO DO YOU THINK YOU ARE?

I would never claim to be the classiest, most confident, most character-driven girl on the planet, but I guarantee I can relate to just about anything you're going through right now: being bullied, being THE bully, insecurity, tragedy, eating disorders, toxic relationships, dating violation, chronic people pleasing, mistakes, embarrassment, depression, parent's divorce, jealousy, never feeling pretty enough, smart enough, funny enough, or enough! The good news is, I have learned to love and respect myself—quirks, challenges, and all.

In this book, I will give you tools that I use daily. I know they can help you, too. When (not *if*) you face challenges in your life, you need tools to be able to pick yourself up and move forward.

HERE'S WHAT YOU CAN EXPECT AS YOU READ:

- 12 chapters of different skills that can help you become the freaking coolest version of yourself.

- 23 science-based tools with a quick reference at the back of book.

- Ridiculous videos at the beginning of each chapter that will give you behind-the-scenes info, as well as additional ideas that can help you rock your universe. (Download any free QR code app now!)

- "Tales of Adventure" (a.k.a. crazy stories from my life). You will get to know me pretty darn well—probably better than you want to. 😊

- Science-based journaling activities. Whip out your fuchsia glitter pen and get ready to get to know yourself even better than you do right now!

Throughout this book, I will share some scientific facts and statistics, but I'll also give you my opinions on just about everything. You are free to disagree with my opinions because they are just that . . . opinions. And I have a lot of them.

HERE ARE MY GOALS FOR THIS BOOK AND FOR YOU:

1 To help you understand what it means to be a real lady: strong, classy, sophisticated, courageous, assertive, tactful, respected, respectful, happy, and confident.

2 To empower you to take control of your life! You have the right to be in the driver's seat of your destiny. Take responsibility and OWN IT.

3 To help you understand your magnanimous worth. You deserve to live a wondrous, happy life!

 OKAY, 9ER 9ER *CHEESE WAGON*—CAPTAIN, OVER.

(Oh, you will want to watch for my CB radio jargon, or "trucker talk" as I like to call it—you'll be fluent by the end of the book—and that's a useful life skill, baby. 😊 When you're through reading, visit TheLostArtofLadyhood.com for a list of all the bizarro definitions. What's the point, you ask? I am the queen of randomness, and trucker talk just makes me laugh.)

Alright ladies, buckle up. Let's go!

SKILL #1

CONFIDENCE

> "THE MOST ATTRACTIVE ACCESSORY A GIRL
> CAN HAVE IS CONFIDENCE."

—AUDREY HEPBURN

 OKAY, BREAKER 1-9, LET'S GET THIS *FREIGHT SHAKER* MOVIN'!

I f you didn't watch the video from the QR code above, you need to. There is a video before each chapter. You can download a free QR code app easily, so you can watch all the videos. I promise my writing craziness will make more sense if you see me in person first . . . in all my insane glory!

Confidence is the foundation for every idea in this book, let me explain why it is so important with my own . . . tales of adventure!

🛼 TALES of ADVENTURE!

"Do you want to be a famous singer, Jessie?" They stared at me with unenthusiastic expressions.

"Are you freaking kidding me?" I shrieked, covering my ear-to-ear grin with both hands over my mouth.

They smiled back at me as if they were watching a five-year-old on Christmas morning.

"We want you to move to Florida to be the next Britney Spears."

I thought hard for about 2.7 seconds before shouting, "Um, like, YES!" Then I packed up my room, signed up for independent study courses (since I was only fifteen and leaving right before my sophomore year of high school), and waved farewell to my family to move across the country to Orlando, Florida—the boy band/Britney Spears–clone capital of the world.

I have been a singer all my life, beginning with twelve straight years of weekly voice lessons, and then working my way up to roaring crowds of seven or eight at county fairs, vocal competitions, forced-smile impromptu renditions at family reunions, all the way to performing for thousands at gigs with my band. I had dreamed of being famous my entire life. I spent way too much time looking at magazines, watching TV, and studying all the great performers: Whitney Houston, Celine Dion, Faith Hill . . . my heroes! From what I could tell by the glossy pages and absolutely FACTUAL media coverage, they all had one thing in common—HAPPINESS! And I honestly thought, with my wide-eyed innocence, that if you're famous, or, more importantly, have your face on Frisbees, t-shirts, and yo-yos (if you indeed had a Frisbee face) you must automatically be happy. Because what could ever go wrong in a world with glamour, beauty, money, and notoriety? NOTHING, that's what. And I wanted it. All of it.

When I first arrived in Florida with my best friends, four boys that were also on this adventure with me, it was everything we hoped it would be. We lived in a beautiful plantation-style home. There was a lake in the backyard, complete with two jet-skis. We were singing in a multi-million dollar recording studio, working with an amazing producer, and dancing with the actual choreographer from the Mickey Mouse Club! M.I.C.K.E.Y. And the best part? Anytime I wanted to go shopping, they would simply hand me a credit card! Are you kidding me? That was when I knew I had arrived. I was living the dream . . . the pop singing, hip-hop dancing, hardworking, performing in front of adoring fans dream.

Within only two months, though, something weird started to happen. My dream began to lose its sparkle. I began sleeping in later and later. One morning in particular, I remember rolling over groggily and looking at the clock: 12:23 p.m., the sun shining straight above. Then I rolled over and went back to sleep! I was supposed to be in the amazing multi-million dollar recording studio that day, and I would rather sleep? What the crap? It happened several more times before I really started to analyze what was going on. I wasn't excited to record my voice.

I wasn't excited to dance. I wasn't excited about my dream. The happiness was getting hazy. I chastised myself—*It's only been two months, Jessie! Are you seriously going to be such a lazy, ungrateful brat and not do your best out here? Now get your patooty out of bed, and get moving!* (And, yes, patooty is a word.)

Over the next few weeks, I tried my best to give one hundred percent. I didn't tell anyone how sluggish I felt—just slapped a smile on my face and got to work. But, as I went about my various activities, I did start to notice some . . . things.

Things like, *Wow. They sure want me to wear skimpy outfits. I really don't want to wiggle into that shrink-wrapped tube top.*

And, *Wow. These lyrics they want me to sing are disgusting. I'm only fifteen! Don't they know how uncomfortable these words are for me?*

And, *Wow. They really want me to dance like that? That's just nasty! Come on, people, I don't even like watching other people dance like that, let alone doing it myself!*

One of the hardest parts was my manager. We shall call him . . . Boris. Boris was the one paying the bill, which meant that I had to make sure I was effusive with gratitude, at all times, for everything he was doing for me. It also came with an understanding that if Boris commanded me to find the cure for cancer while setting a record for longest pogo-stick jump and frying an egg on my forehead, well then, I was expected to do just that. Now, I am an independent little spitfire and proud of it, thus, one day, I decided to dye my hair a fiery red. I was dripping with awesomeness! It was temporary, and could be washed out within a week or two, but I had made one mighty error in judgment! I did not ask permission. I was unaware that something so menial needed to be approved. When Boris saw my hair, he went ballistic! He started screaming—not just raising his voice, but SCREAMING—as only a six-foot, 250-pound, darling fiesta of fun can do.

"HOW DARE YOU DYE YOUR HAIR WITHOUT ASKING ME FIRST! YOU DON'T DO ANYTHING WITHOUT RUNNING IT BY ME! DO YOU HAVE ANY IDEA HOW MUCH MONEY I'VE SPENT ON YOU? YOU UNGRATEFUL LITTLE $%&!" The man spat the swear-word symbols at me. It was like an ice ball to my face, waking me up to what this dream was costing me.

Boris also owned a nightclub—surprise, surprise—or more precisely, a disgusting bar filled with crusty, filthy, drunken old men and greasy fried chicken. The boys and I would perform, hang out, and eat there. Now, when you're fifteen, and you've never been away from home and are still a little naïve, you don't realize what you might be getting yourself into when you enter a prestigious venue such as this. It's kind of like handing a baby a bag of glass shards. Basically, the equation goes something like this: cute teenage girl in skimpy clothes + drunken, lecherous old men = a very frightening situation. I was getting hit on by guys in their sixties. That's the age difference between a grandpa and his grandchild, which translates into really, really nauseating. I still get sick when I think about it.

I felt like a Barbie doll—they dressed me and told me what to sing, how to dance, what to say in interviews, and even what my future was going to be based on how it would benefit them. To be honest, it scared me. I hated the feeling of being controlled . . . of not being ME anymore.

More and more, the thoughts were swirling in my head—*I want to decide what my future will be. I don't want someone else to live my life for me. IT'S MY LIFE*! Even all these years later, I'm getting a little worked up just writing this. I felt suffocated and claustrophobic. By this time, I absolutely knew that fame was not going to be my eternal source of happiness like I had thought. In fact, I had never been more miserable in my entire life, and I had only been on this little excursion for four months! This was the first depression I had ever experienced, and I hated it. Everything was crazy, and though I never imagined I'd feel this way, I knew I had to get out of there.

I went home to Utah to take a break. My family was happy to see me, but I was ECSTATIC to see them! What is it about being around people that you love and who love you, people that you're safe with, and who breathe life into you? I don't know . . . but there's some real awesome sauce in there somewhere. Family rocks!

I spent a lot of time thinking about my options. Do I stay in Utah, giving up on my dream of doing what I love, but be happy? Or do I go back to Florida to stick it out and try to become famous, becoming more and more miserable as I allow someone else to tell me how to live? Though it may not seem like it should have been, it was a difficult decision. Remember, this was my dream for as long as I could remember. In the end, I chose happiness over fame and fortune. I walked away from the record deal.

And I know what you're thinking—*Why didn't she just stand up for herself and not let them control her?* That's an excellent question, and I am glad you asked. The answer to this is why I am writing this book. It is why I am so very passionate about what I do for a living now, and it's also the reason why I deeply care about you . . . whoever you are, rich or poor, old or young, a Pisces or a Leprechaun-lovin' Irishman. If you're reading this and you have any interest in becoming the best version of YOU, then I have an interest in helping you become just that.

Back to the question of why did I not just stand up for myself? The answer is . . . CONFIDENCE.

Or, in my case, a LACK of confidence. While I was in Florida, I wasn't strong enough to say, "NO, I will not wear that miniskirt." "NO, I will not sing those sick lyrics." "NO, I will not ask permission to dye my hair." I didn't value myself enough to take a stand and simply say, "NO." I allowed myself to be controlled because of my insecurities. It was crippling. Self-doubt is the boil on the backside of humanity, and it always leads to misery. It ticks me off, actually. And it's tricky, too, because it's not like a light switch that can easily be turned off and on. It takes time, practice, and strength to drop-kick those feelings of powerlessness out of your life.

Since those early years, I have become a very earnest student of self-confidence. I study it, dream about it, try to practice it, and now—teach it. Not because I think I'm an expert, but because I genuinely wish someone would have taught me the things I'm about to share with you when I needed them most . . . as a teenager.

It is essential that, if you are feeling low, you realize YOU ARE NOT ALONE. Here are some cray-cray statistics about self-esteem from DoSomething.org[1]:

- Low self-esteem is a thinking disorder in which an individual views him/herself as inadequate, unworthy, unlovable, and/or incompetent. Once formed, this negative view of self permeates every thought, producing faulty assumptions and ongoing self-defeating behavior.

- Among high school students, 44 percent of girls and 15 percent of guys are attempting to lose weight.

- Over 70 percent of girls age fifteen to seventeen avoid normal daily activities, such as attending school, when they feel bad about their looks.

- 75 percent of girls with low self-esteem reported engaging in negative activities like cutting, bullying, smoking, drinking, or disordered eating. This compares to 25 percent of girls with high self-esteem who engage in the same negative activities.

- About 20 percent of teens will experience depression before they reach adulthood.

- Teen girls that had a negative view of themselves were four times more likely to take part in activities with boys that they ended up regretting later.

- 7 in 10 girls believe that they are not good enough or don't measure up in some way, including their looks, performance in school, and relationships with friends and family members.

- A girl's self-esteem is more strongly related to how she views her own body shape and body weight, than how much she actually weighs.

I promise you this book is filled with practical applications, not simpering, feel-good platitudes. Confidence is the most important level of all the 12 Skills of Ladyhood, and it will be woven throughout this book. **Confidence is your foundation.** I get so excited because these techniques have been beyond valuable to me as I've worked to battle my own insecurities. It is as simple as the difference between standing in front of the mirror screaming, "Aaaaaahh! Oh, Jessie, DO NOT go outside today—you will frighten children!" and, "Okay, Jessie, today I choose to have a great day!" I have LEARNED to be confident, and I'm pretty psyched about it—so much so that I now feel CONFIDENT enough to share with you these simple concepts and ideas that have absolutely changed my life!

Anytime I have a science-based, real-life technique that psychologists with PhDs actually use to help their patients, I will call it a "tool." These are all aids you can use when you're struggling, or when you need to make a decision, or when you just need help figuring out how you feel about something. There is also a complete list of these tools in the back of the book for future reference.

 OKAY, HERE WE GO ON THE *ZIPPER*, WAKE UP *WILLY WEAVER*, 9ER, OVER!

 TOOL #1

Fake It Till You Make It!

Hypothetical Situation #1: Let's pretend you're sitting on a park bench watching people pass by. You see a beautiful young lady with long brown hair wearing a red shirt and jeans. She is clutching her books to her chest; she's walking quickly with eyes pointed down at the ground. Her shoulders are slumped forward. She is constantly tucking her hair behind her ears and looking around her with darting glances. Do you have that image in your mind? What would your assessment of this girl be? What is she all about? Remember that you don't know this person at all. Scared? Insecure? Anxious, you say? Okay. So, you're telling me that just by the way this girl is walking, the way she carries her shoulders, and how she holds her head, you think she is an insecure person? Interesting!

Hypothetical Situation #2: Same park bench, but now you see a different girl. She's wearing a neon green top and striped leggings. She is looking straight forward, walking swiftly but surely, a slight grin on her face, and her shoulders are pulled back so that she is standing tall. What do you think this girl is like on the inside?

Happy? Strong? Fun? Confident? That's also an interesting observation. So, you're telling me that just by how she carries herself, you think she is confident? Fascinating! Okay, one last question. You think this girl LOOKS confident, but what if she really isn't? What if she is really thinking to herself, *I hope I don't trip down this sidewalk. Maybe I shouldn't even go to my next class—I'm just gonna fail it 'cuz I'm such an idiot. Is that guy looking at me? He's probably shuddering at the sight of my asymmetrical ear lobes . . .* So she's thinking these very destructive thoughts, right? Would you still believe she is a confident person? Of course you would! You don't know what she's thinking, so how would you know the difference? You wouldn't—plain and simple. **Perception is reality.** If you carry yourself confidently and ACT confidently, no one will know whether you really are or aren't! This is called "Fake it till you make it."

Ask yourself these questions? Do you like the way she carries herself? Is that kind of confidence a good quality . . . an attractive quality? Is this a person you would want to hang out with? Is this how you would like to be seen by others? Do you feel like there's a part of you that's hidden from the world? A confident, bold, awesome, funny, relaxed part of you? If so, think about this idea. I'm not telling you to be anything less than authentic—I'm telling you that you have permission to TRY to be the person you want to be! You have permission to bring that bold, happy, strong part of you out of that box you've hidden it in and let it become your everyday self!

I double-dog dare you to try this. If you do and you give it one hundred percent, I promise two things will happen. One, you will be SHOCKED at how easy it is to fool people. And two, you will be equally as SHOCKED to discover how easy it is to become truly confident. You will really start to like yourself. You will discover how strong you are. You will discover how happy you can be if you let the real you shine like the star you are! I strongly believe that if you fake it till you make it, over time, you will BECOME confident simply because you will learn that people will treat you the way you represent yourself. If you choose to pull your shoulders back, walk tall, and slap a smile on your face (even if that's not how you feel) people will treat you accordingly. They will treat you as if you are a confident person. I triple-dog dare you to try it. It will shock you, and it will be a fun experiment. I know it shocked me when I first tried it. It works! Give it a whirl. This one exercise changed my life, and I still use it today when I'm in new, scary situations.

When I was a little girl, I was insecure, not one of the "pretty girls," a total mess in every sense of the word, and very annoyingly dramatic as a means to get attention. As I grew into an adult, I was scared that people would see through me and see that little girl. The truth is, they won't. They don't. People only see what's on the outside. Fake it till you make it . . . and you WILL make it—and sooner than you think! **Confidence is like a muscle; the more you exercise it, the stronger it gets!**

Still not convinced? Here's one more idea to tip the scale for you. Think of your favorite pop star, author, or actor. Someone I admire very much is J. K. Rowling, the author of the brilliant Harry Potter series. (You need to know that I have a small obsession with those books and movies.) So, let's imagine your amazing actor, pop star, or J. K. Rowling getting into a situation where she is completely out of her comfort zone. Let's say Ms. Rowling has been asked to be the keynote speaker at a high school graduation in the Bronx. She is totally out of her element and is feeling really, really, ready-to-throw-up kind of nervous. How do you think J. K. Rowling would walk into that room? Do you think she would be fidgeting with her hair or biting her lip or looking down and hunched over? NO! She would OWN that room within five minutes—I guarantee it! She would walk in there and become the master of New York City. She would CHOOSE to be confident.

I'll say it again, confidence is like a muscle; the more you exercise it, the stronger it becomes.

FOR THE CHRONIC PEOPLE PLEASER

One vital aspect of confidence is standing up for yourself. Learning how to ask for what you want and to say, "No," to what you don't want in a classy, tactful, yet firm way is a fine art, and few are naturally good at it. All my life I have suffered from an affliction called . . . PEOPLE PLEASING. I was always so concerned about looking or being perfect and making those around me happy that I allowed myself to get into some pretty unpleasant situations that taught me some painful lessons.

This is about to get real. I'm going to tell you something that's very personal, something I never really thought I would talk about. It's something that deeply affected me (and my confidence), creating a lot of shame, guilt, and insecurity. It wasn't until I started writing this book that I even remembered the experience. I'm pretty sure I had blocked it out and kept it hidden so I didn't have to face it. It was very strange to me that I had three very vivid dreams of this experience, and it was almost as if I was being sent a message that it was time to face it. My hope in following that message is that someone reading this book will learn something from my story and avoid the same mistake. As I write this, I realize the wisdom in that message because we have to be brave enough to face our past and process our experiences and emotions in healthy ways. Otherwise, we can become bitter and angry, and we don't allow ourselves to heal.

There is no classy way to talk about abuse, and I am filled with fear as I write this. That's why I want to talk about this, but I want you to know where my heart is. I do not talk about this with anger or revengeful thoughts. With all that said, I am consciously choosing to push through the fear and open this important conversation. The whole point I really want you to grasp is that we can't be confident unless we let go of the past, forgive ourselves, and allow ourselves to move forward.

TALES *of* ADVENTURE!

Here goes . . .

When I was fifteen, I hung out with a bunch of guy-friends. I always had a hard time making and keeping girl-friends, so I hung out with boys instead. One of these boys was a very good friend of mine. We hung out a lot and had a good time together. Neither of us were attracted to each other at all, so it really was just a friendship. But one night we were watching a movie together, and out of nowhere he began to touch me very inappropriately. He was making it seem like a joke because he was laughing and teasing with me, but to me, it wasn't a joke. I felt very uncomfortable. I won't go into detail, but it went on for quite some time after that night in different circumstances and got progressively worse. It continued to the point where I was concerned that he would hurt me physically. The point is that my body was mistreated, and I didn't have the confidence to say, "No." I was much more concerned about pleasing him than I was about protecting my body.

I know that's a little heavy to hear right off the bat, and I promise this book won't be depressing like that all the way through. I only share that very personal story because I need you know that you are not alone in your struggles. I know that you, you lovely lady reading this, have experienced pain in your past. Maybe it wasn't as serious as abuse; maybe you have been hurt by your friends, or your parents have divorced, or you feel lonely, or you struggle with your weight/acne/learning disorder/

depression/etc. Or maybe your experience is much worse than mine, and you are struggling big-time with a lot of hurt from your childhood. We have all been through hard things, and we will continue to go through hard things. That's what life is about: finding the strength to get through those storms and loving ourselves enough to let go of our painful past. We need to LEARN to get help, to forgive, and to move forward toward our bright, dazzling futures.

That is what confidence is—learning to love ourselves.

Ready for another tool? Here is my promise, girls: if you will really think about the tools in this book and how they can help YOUR life, things will get easier for you—not easy, but easier, because you have some knowledge of how to handle the curve balls of life. I know because I've been there, and I have done the work to help you get there, too.

 TOOL #2

People Pleaser Check-In!

People pleasing really is one thing that can destroy you and your confidence. I even see adults who struggle with this. Since I have experienced so much pain and discomfort from my chronic pleasing disease, I know firsthand how dangerous it is. So, address it now so you can prevent painful lessons down the road. There is no way you can become a confident lady of awesomeness if you are a chronic pleaser.

HERE IS YOUR PLEASER QUIZ. CIRCLE THE BEST ANSWER, AND BE HONEST WITH YOURSELF.

Do you say "no" to your friends when they want to catch that stupid horror movie you don't want to see?

YES   NO   SOMETIMES

When your friend asks for the twelfth straight day if she can borrow a dollar for the vending machine, do you give it to her?

YES   NO   SOMETIMES

When your boyfriend wants to make out, do you decide beforehand where you will draw the line of how far to go?

YES   NO   SOMETIMES

Your older brother is supposed to babysit your baby sister but at the last minute he bails and tells you to watch her. Do you let him go and do the babysitting?

YES   NO   SOMETIMES

Your mom pushes you really hard to play the violin. You hate it and you know 100 percent for certain that you don't want to continue with it, but you keep playing because you feel guilty about all the money she has spent. Do you continue rather than talk to your mom about it?

YES   NO   SOMETIMES

Suzie Loo (the queen bee of your group) starts gossiping about Lily. You are friends with Lily. She is saying very mean things that you know are not true. Do you defend Lily?

YES   NO   SOMETIMES

You know your math teacher is going to chew you out for not turning an important assignment in on time. Do you make up a hugely elaborate, completely untrue story about how you had to go to the emergency room because you thought you had appendicitis or some equally ridiculous lie to avoid her anger?

YES   NO   SOMETIMES

If taking that quiz made you realize that you might be a people pleaser, good news—there is hope! And it doesn't even require rehab. It just requires awareness and courage to change.

Many people pleasers struggle because they just don't know how to say "No." Let's all pinky swear right now that when sticky situations come up, we will tell ourselves to be brave and say "NO."

🔩 TOOL #3

5 Great Ways to Say "No"

1   "No." The word *no* is a complete sentence. You don't have to explain, justify, or rationalize. You don't have to even have a reason.

2   Walk away. You can just ignore it, and by doing so can send a strong message.

3   "My mom won't let me." Trust me, your parents will be happy to have you blame them if you need to get out of a hard situation.

4   Use humor. Make a joke out of it. "I have to floss my cat," or "I'm just too busy practicing my kazoo."

5   Complete honesty. "I don't feel comfortable with that," or "That freaks me out," or "I just don't like that idea, sorry." Complete honesty is great because you will be majorly exercising your confidence muscle.

 TOOL #4

DRAGON WARRIOR

Kung Fu Panda is one of my favorite movies of all time. My daughter and I take karate together, and I have a five-year-old son who is already showing a lot of promise as a Kung Fu Fighter (a.k.a.—beating down his older sister with plastic toys). I think I've watched the movie about 746 times, and now I'm craving "secret ingredient soup." And since we're on the subject, I can think of no better object lesson for this chapter than *Kung Fu Panda*. Beware—there are spoilers if you haven't seen it.

The movie starts out with an adorable yet awkward panda bear named Po. Po dreams of being a Kung Fu master, but everyone around him tells him that he doesn't have what it takes. Then, something amazing happens. Master Oogway (a slow-moving turtle who just happens to have wicked Kung Fu skills) chooses Po to become the "Dragon Warrior," the most powerful Kung Fu fighter of all. It takes the entire movie for Po to realize that all he has to do is CHOOSE to believe that he IS the Dragon Warrior.

Now, you have to know that Po's dad makes the famous "secret ingredient soup." This is the best, most delicious noodle soup in the world. At the very moment Po is about to give up on ever becoming the Dragon Warrior, he learns the secret of the "secret ingredient soup."

"Nothing!" his dad tells him. "There is no secret ingredient."

Po realizes there is no magic ingredient that is going to change him into the Dragon Warrior, either! He understands he already has what it takes, and he chooses to believe. When he makes that choice, he is able to defeat the villain, Tai Lung. All he needed to unleash his greatness was to believe in himself. Was he still the awkward, shy, ridiculous noodle maker? Yep! But he discovered that there was MORE to him than that—and he OWNED it!

I know *Kung Fu Panda* is just a cartoon, but it illustrates such a beautiful truth: we have the choice to see our awesomeness and to live great lives. **Choosing to believe in your greatness is yet another tool you can use to build your confidence.**

Now run and grab your favorite glow-in-the-dark, neon pen. This book is sprinkled with places to record your thoughts and

ideas. No skipping the homework, ladies—let's journal! Here
are some questions to help you build your confidence muscle.

🖉 JOURNAL TIME

What scares you?

_____

_____

_____

What's the worst thing that would happen if you
faced these fears?

_____

_____

_____

Weighing the risks, would it be worth it to work
through these fears?

_____

_____

_____

What happens if you don't work past those fears?

_____

_____

_____

Make a plan to summon your inner Dragon Warrior and conquer one of your fears.

_____

_____

_____

_____

_____

_____

_____

_____

_____

_____

_____

_____

_____

_____

_____

BUILD YOUR FOUNDATION

The point of these tools and stories is to help you realize that confidence can be learned! FamilyEducation.com says that in order for you to become strong and feel good about yourself, you need three things[2]:

1   To get to know yourself well

2   To think of yourself as capable

3   To believe you can measure up to others' expectations

Learning confidence can help you work toward these three things. **Confidence is the foundation for your life.** You can build a monumental, majestic, beautiful skyscraper, but without a solid foundation, it will crumble. Learn to love yourself first, then you can truly build something great. And, honey, you were meant for greatness!

 I DARE YA, *DISCO LIGHTS* . . .

CONFIDENT, CLASSY LADIES CHOOSE CONFIDENCE.

♡ CHALLENGE

Choose to be confident for one week. Just see what kind of magic happens! . . . it all comes down to our choices.

WRITE ABOUT YOUR EXPERIENCE:

_____

_____

_____

_____

_____

_____

_____

_____

LEADERSHIP

> "Leaders are the creators of their lives.
> Followers let life happen to them."
>
> —UNKNOWN

I believe there are two types of people in this world . . . breathers and suckers. One of my mentors, a rock star author and motivational speaker, Josh Shipp (HeyJosh.com), told me, "Some people have the power to breathe life into you, and some people can suck the life right out of you." Do you want to be a breather or a sucker? Well I don't know about you, but I have experienced mean people, and I don't want to be like them. I want to be a breather, and I only want to hang out with breathers. Another word for a breather is a leader.

My guess is that if you're reading this book you aren't the kind of person who wants to settle for average. I'm glad because I'm here to tell you the world NEEDS you to strive for excellence!

We need remarkable leaders, and you could be a great leader if you are willing to do the work! You can't get anywhere without hard work.

Leadership is not just about being a CEO of a big company or being the person that always gives advice and is naturally seen as a "wise" person. It's about using your abilities and light to influence other people in positive ways. It's about being kind and helping other people feel good about who they are. It's about making an effort to build other people up and to help them make good decisions. It's about setting an example and trying to live your life in such a way that you can be seen as a role model. That is what real leadership is.

WHAT IS HOLDING YOU BACK?

I know what you're thinking, *I'm not a leader, Jessie. I've made too many mistakes,* or *I'm too much of a mess,* or *I'm just not a good enough person to be any kind of an example.* I hear you, and I know exactly what you mean! The good news is that you don't have to be perfect to be a leader. Let's talk about a few things that may be holding you back from being the awesome leader you can be.

One common mental road block is thinking that you are not perfect, so you just can't be a good leader. I know how it feels to NOT feel good enough to be a leader, let me share a short story.

👢 TALES *of* ADVENTURE!

A month after turning sixteen and getting my driver's license, I was driving home from a road trip with my brother and looked behind me to see red and blue flashing lights. I just about had a heart attack and starting sobbing immediately. I was being pulled over for the first time. Did I mention I'd only had my license for one month? So depressing!

"Do you have any idea how fast you were going just now, little lady?" (He actually called me "little lady." Right out of a John Wayne cowboy movie.)

"No," I cried. (Bawl, sob, cry, escalate to ugly cry, sob).

"110 miles per hour," he stated coldly, looking right through my soul.

"Are you kidding me?" I was too shocked to cry anymore.

The price of that ticket was more than I made in three months at my minimum-wage job, and the embarrassment of telling my parents was excruciating.

I wish I could tell you that was the extent of my bad driving, but that would be a lie. It only gets worse! Within nine years, I had a grand total of eleven speeding tickets, I had been to traffic school four times, I was responsible for three car accidents (fender benders—no one was hurt, but they were my fault), and I had my license suspended for having too many points on my driving record. Yikes! And, yes, it's really embarrassing for me to tell you all of that, but it's important that you know *I* need to do these exercises, too!

So, if you don't remember anything else from this book, I want you to remember these two things: ALWAYS obey the speed limit, and forgive yourself for the mistakes you've made.

Even though I still feel a sting when I think about my less-than-stellar driving record, I have let go of the guilt and shame. I used to cry over it and be scared out of my mind to get behind the wheel! Now, it still makes me uncomfortable, but I'm able to just get on with life because I have let it go, forgiven myself, and put a lot of effort into driving as carefully as I can.

It didn't happen overnight; it was a process. This isn't a quick fix. It takes dedication and strength to own your life. But when I made the decision to stop holding myself back, I was able to not feel terrified of getting behind the wheel of a car just because I had made mistakes. Indeed . . . many, many mistakes. ☺

If we can learn to forgive ourselves for the mistakes, embarrassments, self-defeating behaviors, regrets, break-ups, and just the overall pain we have experienced in our lives, then we can find our inner leader.

On the site PsychologyToday.com (which I totally love because I am a psychology nut), Steve Baskin, owner of Camp Champions, says:

> Leading is more about learning specific skills than possessing inherent qualities. In this way, being a leader is like being an athlete. Certainly, some children are born with attributes that aid in athletics, such as size and quick reflexes. But success in athletics requires thousands of hours of practice to acquire the skills needed for success.

Ultimately, success has much more to do with the skills honed through practice than genetics. Leadership is important; it involves a series of skills, and these skills require practice. Teens who wish to develop and hone their leadership acumen should seek out opportunities to work with groups of younger children to get this practice. If they do so, they'll be pleased to learn how easily these skills can be transferred to leadership in all areas of their lives.[1]

TOOL #5

Identify Self-Defeating Behaviors

Think about ways you hold yourself back or deny yourself the happiness you deserve. When we engage in self-defeating behaviors, we are working against ourselves. It is like kicking a soccer ball into your own goal. Bad idea. Here were some of my self-defeating actions and thoughts before I started owning my life:

- I judge, gossip, and criticize others.

- I criticize and beat myself up when I make a tiny mistake.

- I don't stand up for family or friends (or even people I don't know).

- I don't forgive myself.

- I don't forgive others.

- I am not confident enough to feel okay about myself without someone else validating me with a compliment.

- I procrastinate.

✏ JOURNAL TIME

Now it's your turn. Grab a purple marker and list your self-defeating behaviors.

_____

_____

_____

_____

_____

_____

_____

_____

_____

_____

_____

TIME TO FIND THAT LEADER

Now that we have recognized some possible roadblocks, let's look at some ways to find the leader that is right inside you. Leadership is such a beautiful character trait because it is an emotional boost. Think of a time where you felt like you helped someone make a good decision, built someone up with a compliment or encouragement, or made a good choice that you think set a good example for someone else. Picture that specific moment in time, and then check in with how you feel right now. Those memories should create feelings of pride, excitement, and happiness—proof that you are a powerful leader, whether you feel like you are or not.

Let's look at some awesome leaders from history who exercised that leadership muscle and are perfect examples of "breathers." Some of my favorite leaders are Audrey Hepburn, a woman who was a star on the silver screen but also cherished her role as a mother and ambassador for UNICEF; Benjamin Franklin, one of our founding fathers, who is a perfect example of how you can become great as long as you're willing to work for it; Princess Diana, another woman who could have used her fame to just live a leisurely life, but instead tirelessly worked at serving those around her; Oprah, a beautiful, generous, ambitious leader; Celine Dion, an amazing mother and dreamer (and my singing hero!); Carol Burnett, a brave woman who paved her own road in comedy—starring in the highly successful *Carol Burnett Show*. And my new favorite is Jennifer Lawrence from *The Hunger Games*!

Let's talk about Jennifer, since she's one of my favorite actresses. At the time I'm writing this, *Catching Fire* just came out and J-Law is glorious! I'm sure you love her as much as I do. Her humor, confidence, and down-to-earth personality is contagious. She is so real! One of my favorite Jennifer Lawrence quotes is when she gave her opinion about The Hunger Games movies: "Don't go see the movies, I'm a troll. I think the movie was great, but their biggest mistake was me."[2]

This is a girl that rocks that silver screen, but I actually believe her when she shares this thought about herself. For us normal humans, we can't begin to imagine why! This is a great example of that "Fake It Till You Make It" idea. Here she is, totally awesome, but unaware of how awesome she is. Here's me just geeking out about how fabulous she is, feeling very inspired and motivated to pursue my dreams because of the example she has set while pursuing hers. That's a lot of awesomeness. She's a leader, without being "perfect." We all have that kind of power in us.

Another random quote, just for the fun of it:

"I'm a horrible dancer! I'm like a dad at prom. I look like Gumby getting electrocuted."

—JENNIFER LAWRENCE

It's important to note here that you don't have to be anything near a celebrity to be a leader. You don't need a platform that reaches thousands or even one hundred. If you can positively influence ONE person's life, you are a leader. Maybe that one person is your younger sister who looks up to you because you are really good in school; or maybe it's your next door neighbor, who appreciates your example because you are kind to your parents, and he has a hard time with his parents, so your example motivates him to try harder; maybe it's your math teacher, who appreciates your leadership skills when you tell everyone to quiet down and listen to him teach. You never know who you just might inspire . . . you may never know. That is the whole point of leadership. You don't make good choices because you want people to notice; you do it because it's right, and THAT is what people notice.

Think of yourself as a seed planter. You just be the best leader you can be. Look at the bigger picture—even if people don't appreciate those compliments you give, or see that you're making hard decisions and trying to be a good person, you are planting seeds. Even just planting a few seeds will benefit YOU in so many ways. This is sounding a lot like that one thing—oh, it's on the tip of my tongue! What is it? Oh, yes, INTEGRITY. This is a big word that can change your life for the better. It means to be honest with yourself. When we can be honest with ourselves and do what we know is right, we have integrity. And that is always a good thing.

Here are some real-life stories from teens like you who have made the brave choice to find their inner leader. As you're reading, think about this: if you had a five-year-old tell you that you were their hero, how would that affect the way you act every day?

"I was a leader when I decided to stop yelling at my younger brother for bugging me all the time and decided to just play with him for a little while. That's all he needed, and now he knows I love him but he doesn't need to be with me all the time. And now I don't feel so bad for always being mean to him."

—OLIVIA, AGE 14

"I was a leader when I stood up to my friend for gossiping about our other friend, Mikenna. I told her to be nice because I wouldn't want stuff like that said about me."

—LEENA, AGE 16

"I was a leader when I noticed my mom getting really stressed out at my older sisters, so I told them to all calm down and be nice to mom, because she is about to lose it."

—SARAH, AGE 12

"I was a leader when I told Connor to stop talking in our history class. I told him to be more respectful because our teacher was too nice to get mad, but I could tell Connor was driving him crazy."

—CAMI, AGE 13

"I was a leader at my church when I suggested a fun service project where we could make cookies for our garbage men in our neighborhood and make big posters saying "Thank You!" and attach them to the garbage cans. All the girls in

my group thought that would be fun, but we're still deciding where to leave the cookies so they don't get thrown away."

—MALLORY, AGE 17

Can you hear the excitement and confidence as these girls share? Here is the reason why: As we lift and build others, part of the payback is that we, too, are lifted—CONFIDENCE BOOST! Being a leader allows us to build ourselves, too!

 **TOOL #6**

Leadership Hunt

I believe we are all born with natural leadership, but sometimes we just have to go a-hunting for it. Write down some ideas of ways you can find the leader that I know YOU know is inside you. This may sound funny, but before we can be good leaders for others, we need to be a good leader in our own life. So—the first step is YOU!

 JOURNAL TIME

Polka dot pencil call—let's go!

How can I be a better leader within myself? Think about having more integrity, being honest, being kinder to myself, having better self-discipline, setting a new goal, etc.

Now it's time to branch out and take a look at how you can be a leader to those all around you. Let's start with those people you see every day.

How can I be a leader in my family?

_____

_____

How can I be a leader in my school?

_____

_____

How can I be a leader with my friends?

_____

_____

CHOOSE TO BE A LEADER

Another important element to leadership is understanding your own personality. I addressed this already, but I want to make sure it's clear that you don't have to be that natural leader, the person who is always making the decisions for the group, or the person everyone goes to for advice, or the person who sets all the new trends. You can be shy, introverted, independent, or have acne-prone skin, or you can be crazy, weird, and hyper, AND you can still be a great leader! Being a leader is a character trait that is a CHOICE—not just a personality trait. Having said that, the people who are natural leaders have a beautiful gift. Some people are just born with leadership skills, and that's awesome, but some of us have to work at it, and that's okay!

One way to tap into our inner leader is to really know ourselves. When we know ourselves well, we feel confident—CONFIDENCE BOOST! We don't need to worry about who we are, but instead we can turn our attention to see what we can do to help someone else.

Take this personality test to learn more about your natural personality. Keep in mind that one personality is never BETTER than another, it is just DIFFERENT. Your natural personality is beautiful. No matter your individual personality, I want it to be clear that when I encourage you to be a leader, I am NOT saying that you should try to push yourself to be someone you're not. My definition of leadership is simply being the best version of you, so you can breathe life into others.

You have to read the book *The Color Code* by Dr. Taylor Hartman. This book helps you make sense of your personality and embrace your natural way of thinking and being. It is just a freaking cool book! There are other personality books out there, but this one is the best.

Here's a little test I created. It will help you see some of your personality traits and give you a quick glimpse into your awesomeness.

PERSONALITY TEST

On a scale of 1 to 3, (1 meaning you strongly agree, 2 meaning maybe or sometimes, and 3 meaning you strongly disagree), are you . . .

Talkative?	1	2	3
Worried?	1	2	3
Funny?	1	2	3
Assertive?	1	2	3
Popular?	1	2	3
Unique?	1	2	3
On time?	1	2	3
Curious?	1	2	3
Goal-oriented?	1	2	3
Reliable?	1	2	3
Energetic all the time?	1	2	3

Happy most the time?   1   2   3

A pleaser?   1   2   3

Academically smart?   1   2   3

Physically healthy?   1   2   3

A shoulder to cry on?   1   2   3

Tense?   1   2   3

Organized?   1   2   3

Hard working?   1   2   3

Creative?   1   2   3

Cold to strangers?   1   2   3

A good listener?   1   2   3

Moody?   1   2   3

Outgoing?   1   2   3

Resilient?   1   2   3

Artistic?   1   2   3

Boring?   1   2   3

Easily distracted?   1   2   3

Lazy?   1   2   3

A hugger?   1   2   3

DO YOU . . .

Compliment others?   1   2   3

Finish the job?   1   2   3

Do the job well?	1	2	3
Get asked for advice?	1	2	3
Let yourself cry?	1	2	3
Start fights?	1	2	3
Eat when stressed?	1	2	3
Trust people?	1	2	3
Like yourself?	1	2	3
Gossip?	1	2	3
Stand up for yourself?	1	2	3

ARE YOU MOST INTERESTED IN (CIRCLE ONE):

A   POPULARITY

B   BEING A "GOOD GIRL"

C   HAVING FUN

D   FEELING PEACE

I'm keeping this really simple. I like the idea of asking yourself these questions to find out how you see yourself. It's also fun to have someone else take the quiz with you in mind. We can learn so much about who we are and who we want to be by asking ourselves questions and by journaling—hence all the journaling exercises you'll find in this book.

Check out these websites for more comprehensive personality tests:

- Queendom.com (You have to buy your test scores, but they're worth it for $6!)
- SimilarMinds.com
- OutofService.com
- PsychCentral.com

THE ART OF LADYHOOD AND LEADERSHIP IS ALL ABOUT BREATHING LIFE INTO OTHERS.

 CHALLENGE

Exercise your leadership muscle for one week! Pick one idea you journaled about in Tool #4: Leadership Hunt, and focus on that for one week. Keep in mind that leadership is something we can always be working on. We don't have to be perfect to be leaders, we just have to choose to try . . . it all comes down to our choices.

WRITE ABOUT YOUR EXPERIENCE:

_____

_____

_____

_____

_____

_____

_____

_____

_____

_____

GRATITUDE

"THE SINGLE GREATEST THING YOU CAN DO TO CHANGE
YOUR LIFE TODAY, IS TO START BEING GRATEFUL FOR
WHAT YOU HAVE RIGHT NOW."

—OPRAH WINFREY

Have you ever thought, *I wish I had a cuter clothes*, or *I wish I had thinner thighs*, or *I wish I was more popular*, or *I wish I was smarter—I'm so bad at math*, or *I wish my family was richer*, or *I wish Johnny in my English class would notice me*? I wish . . . I wish . . . I wish . . . If we spend our lives wishing and hoping for the things we want but don't have, that is the quickest path to misery! However, if we choose to focus on and even LOOK for the good, happy, positive, awesome, wondrous things in our lives . . . THAT is a pretty quick path to a breathtaking, remarkable, splendid experience on this earth! Gratitude can get us there.

TALES of ADVENTURE!

When I was seventeen, I heard about an audition for a Broadway touring company, and I thought, *Blah. I'm too tired. Plus, it's probably not even a real play. I bet it's one of those dinner theater things.* Well, lucky for me, I had a great friend named Ben (shout out) who told me to get ready, because he was coming to get me. He gave me no choice. I was going to the audition. Thank heaven for friends who are willing to slap you upside your lazy head.

I'm not really into acting, but I love to dance and sing, so when I got there and found out the show was *Footloose*, I flipped out a little. I loved that movie! That Kevin Bacon . . . nutritious and delicious.

The first dance audition went great, and I got a callback. The second round of the dance portion also went great. They announced the dancers who had made it, and I was on the list! SCREAM! Then came the singing auditions. I made some mistakes, but I still felt okay about it. When the producer called me from her New York office a few days later to let me know that I was being cast as a principle dancer and singer, I'm pretty sure I shrieked right into the phone! I would get to do hip hop dancing, have speaking parts, and sing freaking awesome songs! But that wasn't even half of it!

We would get paid $700 a week (to me that was a fortune!), perform for sold-out concert halls that seated 10,000 or more people, AND we were going to rehearse in New York City for three weeks before starting a four-month tour to thirty-seven states! *HOLY RUSTED METAL, BATMAN! Maybe Broadway is the way I can use my voice and be happy*, I thought. It was such an amazing opportunity, and I was so grateful I went to that audition. I can't believe I almost missed it because I was being lazy.

Now here's something unexpected. One of the cool things I learned during this amazing tour was that Broadway was NOT something I wanted to do. Though I enjoyed the experience immensely and would love to perform in musicals again someday, I discovered that the lifestyle wasn't something I wanted. I spent four months on a tour bus with some of the most amazingly talented, kind, and giving people I had ever met. But, sadly, I watched most of them try to destroy themselves. Drugs and alcohol were used constantly. It was so devastating to watch because these were people who could sing the lights out and dance better than anyone you will ever see on *So You Think You Can Dance*. Yet, they were destroying their instruments and their bodies.

I decided then and there that I did not want to do drugs or drink alcohol. It seriously broke my heart to see those destructive forces hurting my friends. The common denominator with all these incredible people was lack of confidence. Sure, they were dynamic and mesmerizing on stage, but off stage, they didn't have a clue about who they were or what they wanted out of life. They were just existing. I'm not making assumptions, by the way. These amazing people TOLD me they were unhappy. Drugs were their "out." Getting high was an escape from their life. If they only knew there were other, better ways to get happy.

One of those ways is GRATITUDE. I am one hundred percent sure that if these incredibly talented humans could have taken a step back and looked at all the things they had to be grateful for, they could have saved their voices and bodies from all that poison.

Don't do drugs, girls!

It is heartbreaking to watch someone constantly hold themselves back from greatness. Especially when YOU see that greatness in them!

Shooting for our dreams and trying to find our greatness is so awesome because, by just trying, sometimes we will discover we don't actually want what we thought we wanted. Life rarely turns out the way we plan. This can be a good thing. Often, there are better things in store that we couldn't have planned for ourselves. I learned so many things from this experience: I learned that my job is to love my friends, not judge them. I learned that the Broadway life wasn't actually my dream job. I learned to appreciate and take care of my body. And I learned to focus on the good things in life because gratitude helps me feel happy.

Here's some rock-solid science to back me up on the benefits of making the choice to live in gratitude. John Tierney, a reporter for the *New York Times*, interviewed world-renowned psychologists who have dedicated their lives to studying gratitude. He found common threads throughout their studies. Tierney reports, "Cultivating an attitude of gratitude has been linked to better health, sounder sleep, less anxiety and depression, higher long-term satisfaction with life, and kinder behavior toward others . . ."[1]

TOOL #7

GRATITUDE JOURNAL

Dr. Michael E. McCullough from the University of Miami is one of the professors interviewed by John Tierney. Dr. McCullough says that he instructed his test participants to keep a daily journal recording five things they felt grateful for each day. This required them to think and put effort into LOOKING for things to be grateful for—which is a huge part of the reason why this exercise WORKS! The people would write down even the small things like a sunset or learning something new or someone doing something kind for them. At the end of a two-month study, these people were significantly happier and more optimistic about life. They even reported that they felt fewer physical ailments and found that they had more energy to exercise more! That's science, ladies.

No one can argue with these kinds of studies. These types of activities can make a huge difference in your life! Give a gratitude journal a try. Since this is a daily activity, I recommend looking for a separate journal dedicated just to gratitude. You can find cute, classy, and even bedazzled journals at bookstores, or there's pretty shnazzy ones at the dollar store, or go grab a spiral notebook—easy! Just record five things a day for a few weeks, and see how you feel!

GRATITUDE LIST

Taking it one step further, create a gratitude list. I challenge you to think of fifty or even a hundred things that can fuel you when you're feeling low. There is so much power in positive thinking—in fact, I have a whole chapter about that coming up! Gratitude can help us train our minds to see the good things in the world, to have hope, to feel excited about our lives, and to notice the little things.

JOURNAL TIME

What are you grateful for? Now where did you put that pen?

I didn't put any lines here on purpose. Instead of writing in this book, find a loose sheet of paper, and make a nice long list. When you're done, put it where you will see it every single day. Maybe you could tape it onto your bathroom mirror, so you can look at it first thing in the morning, or put it on the dashboard of your car (watch the road though),or tape it to the inside of your school binder so you see it a few times during the day. Here are some ideas to help get you started:

SECRET INGREDIENT SOUP

- Tapioca
- Clean underwear
- Chubby fingers
- Eyesight
- Refrigerated food
- Pogo sticks
- Family
- Pop tarts
- Bendable straws

_____

_____

_____

_____

_____

_____

_____

_____

If we can live in gratitude for the things we do have and not focus on the things we don't, we will be happier. That's a fact! Our hearts will be healthier, our hair will be shinier, and our life will feel fuller. Gratitude is an easy path to happiness.

Dr. Robert Emmons, author of *Thanks!: How Practicing Gratitude Can Make You Happier*, says that in the first major study of gratitude, wanting what we have has been scientifically proven to increase your happiness by 25 percent![2] That's a big deal if you are struggling to get out of bed in the morning . . . and we've all been there. Emmons discovered that if you can keep a gratitude journal, just recording a few things each day that you are grateful for, you can actually improve your sleep and increase energy. That's a pretty powerful tool. If you haven't ever thought about the mind-body connection, it's time. You have more control over your body than you think. Your thoughts are powerful. You've heard, "You are what you eat," right? I'll take it a step further—"You are what you THINK." If you choose to focus your thoughts on things you are grateful for, happiness is a natural byproduct.

When I was a kid, I always hated my fingers. I thought they were so chubby. They looked like little sausages. It sounds so stupid now, but this was a serious source of insecurity for me— weird, I know. Of all the things to be insecure about! One day, a friend of mine was sick and tired of me complaining about my fat fingers (no one likes a complainer . . . very annoying), and she said to me, "Would you rather not have any fingers, Jessie?" I had honestly never thought of that. From then on, I could only think of it like that. Can you imagine your life without your fingers? Scary . . . and hard! Our fingers are amazing with all the different things they do. I would much rather have chubby fingers than no fingers at all. Take a bite out of that cheeseburger for a minute. (That means—think about it.)

 GOT IT, *SKILLET FACE*? DON'T LET THE *SUPER CHICKENS* MOW YOU OVER. OVER AND OUT.

WE CAN RECLAIM THE LOST ART OF LADYHOOD BY ACTIVELY LOOKING FOR THINGS TO BE GRATEFUL FOR!

 CHALLENGE

Choose to live one hundred percent in gratitude for an entire week. This means no complaining, whining, or focusing on the things you DON'T HAVE or the things you DON'T LIKE (chubby fingers). If an ungrateful thought comes into your head, kick it out immediately, and replace it with a grateful thought . . . it all comes down to our choices.

WRITE ABOUT YOUR EXPERIENCE:

_____

_____

_____

_____

_____

_____

_____

_____

_____

SKILL #4

SELF-DEFENSE

Why self-defense isn't taught in public school curriculum—kindergarten through twelfth grade—I'll never know or understand. This is such a vital skill. In this chapter, we will chat about keeping yourself safe, setting concrete personal boundaries, and becoming more aware of the power you have to protect your body.

Just repeat after me: I AM WORTH PROTECTING! I AM WORTH PROTECTING!

👢 TALES of ADVENTURE!

One night, at about 11:30 p.m., I pulled into a self-serve car wash. As soon as I got out of the car, I had an overwhelming feeling to get out of there. Since I'm already scared of the dark (totally true—not ashamed 😊), I decided not to question that feeling. I jumped in my car and sped off as fast as I could. As I was driving away with my heart still pounding in my chest, I started to think, if I was a predator, where would I go to find my prey? And the answer was pretty clear—I would go to a self-serve car wash at 11:30 at night! Cement walls and a lot of shadows . . . perfect hunting grounds. That was a profound moment for me because I remember thinking, *Wow, I am actually connected to my intuition.*

We have been given a wonderful gift, ladies; we can be in tune with ourselves if we take the time to listen and to follow that quiet compass—our own personal Jiminy Cricket. I believe we can be led OUT of the wrong direction and be led IN the right direction if we listen to that intuition.

SELF-DEFENSE MAD SKILLS

Now, onto the topic at hand—SELF-DEFENSE! When it comes to self-defense, I am one of those fanatical, crazy ladies! I'm telling you, someday I am going to Washington, DC, to lobby on Capitol Hill for self-defense education to be standard in public school. It's amazing to me that we are taught calculus, a skill that 98.9 percent of people will never use in their lifetime, but we aren't taught how to defend our bodies! The US Department of Justice tells us that 16- to 19-year-old teens were "3.5 times more likely than the general population to be victims of rape, attempted rape, or sexual assault."[1] It is shocking to me that statistics like this are still not enough to make us take this epidemic seriously as a society.

Education is readily available, and it could literally mean life or death. In my home, I tell my children that there are three things that are not optional: college, piano, and karate. My daughter and I started karate at the same time. She was seven years old; I was twenty-eight. It's been such an incredible experience to learn how to defend ourselves . . . together. Now, obviously, you first start out taking karate because you want to learn self-defense, but it's amazing how much MORE you learn. You learn self-control, respect, discipline, and my favorite . . . confidence! I have learned things that I didn't know I would learn. I thought I would learn skills I could use in case I was attacked by some darkly cloaked man at midnight in a self-serve car wash, but I've also learned how to control my strength, value my safety, and believe in myself.

Self-Defense is so important, especially for girls. We must be strong enough to protect ourselves. The coolest thing I have learned from my education in Chun Kuk Do (the martial arts system designed by Chuck Norris himself!) is that if you walk with confidence, you are much less likely to be attacked in the first place. A predator looks for someone who carries themselves in a way that subliminally says, *I won't fight back*. So if you are walking tall, your shoulders back, a smile on your face, and with strength in your stride, you're already much less likely to be a victim. That fact is very powerful. (Sounds a lot like something we just talked about, right?). Exercise that confidence muscle, girls!

Now, I want to be clear. No one who has been a victim of violence or abuse is to blame for the incident—confidence or no, training or no. Terrible things can happen to anyone; that's just a sad fact of life. We can't control other people's actions, but we can prepare ourselves. I just want you to be as prepared as you possibly can be to face what may or may not come. And remember, it's not just for your physical safety, either. Being prepared is also for your long term emotional and mental happiness.

If you're thinking, *I wish I could take karate lessons, but I don't have any money, Jessie!*, I would suggest calling every single karate studio in your county and offering to trade your time for lessons. That's how seriously I recommend this. You could offer to wash their windows, mop their floors, and take out the trash in exchange for the confidence and priceless knowledge of how to protect yourself in an emergency. That is a very unequal trade in your favor.

Put yourself in the shoes of a person that you know has experienced some kind of violence or abuse. I'm positive you know someone. This affects so many people all over the world—guys and girls! Think about their experience, and think about the aftermath. Put yourself in their shoes, and ask yourself this question: If those people could go back, do you think they would do whatever it took to prepare themselves to fight and defend themselves if they could? The answer is, yes, of course! I know that not all acts of violence can be prevented by knowing how to do a proper jab or solar plexus punch, but if there was even a chance, don't you think your friend would happily take out the trash of a karate studio so that they could learn the skills they needed to avoid that one moment in time when all of their power was taken away? I bet my parakeet they would.

Let me ask the same question in a different way. If you knew that, sometime in your life, you would have to defend yourself, you just knew that was in the deck of cards you were going to be dealt, would you prepare as best you could? Well, since we can't predict our future, all we can do is prepare for the worst and hope for the best. Karate lessons are worth every penny and every minute because YOU are worth protecting.

Watch the video for this chapter to see self-defense techniques in action! In addition to the video, here are a few tips to help get you thinking.

 TOOL #8

Self-Defense Awesomeness

- Many people think of self-defense as a karate kick to the groin or jab in the eyes of an attacker. But self-defense actually means doing everything possible to AVOID fighting someone who threatens or attacks you.

- Self-defense is all about using your smarts—not your fists.

- Most attackers are someone you KNOW! It's rare for some stranger to jump out of the shadows. Statistics show that 82 percent of the women who are raped are victimized by someone they know.[2] Keep this in mind.

- Trust your instincts, and be smart! Avoid being out by

yourself at night in places that could compromise your safety. If your Spidey sense starts tingling and you feel like something is wrong, listen to that feeling, and get out of there!

- If you're getting robbed and the person is asking for your purse, give it to him! You are much more valuable than anything in your wallet. Again, you want to avoid a fight. You just never know if he has a gun, or if he's high on something. Don't risk it unless you absolutely have to!

- Stay calm and breathe. The second you get into a scary situation, your body immediately starts pumping adrenaline throughout your system. Consciously telling yourself to stay calm and breathe will help you think more clearly.

- Make sure you communicate with your family and friends about where you will be at all times.

- SCREAM! Just by throwing a full-on, two-year-old tantrum and making a lot of noise, an attacker will think twice. Say things like, "Police!" "Get away!" "Fire!" "Stop!"

- Brute force is generally not the smartest option. Doing the unexpected is! In other words, HURT HIM! Kick him as hard as you can in the groin, gouge his eyes, bite his arm, stomp on the top of his foot, break his nose, kick his knee, poke his throat, scratch and claw like a wild tiger, pinch his inner thigh (very sensitive)! Do whatever you have to do to save your life! Throw all the "ladylike" ideas out of your head when it comes to protecting yourself.

- Your elbow is the strongest point on your body. If you get close enough, use it. If you end up on the ground, use your legs to kick free from your attacker.

- "No." is a complete sentence. You always have the right to say "No" to someone who is making you uncomfortable.

- Take protective measures: lock your car doors, lock your front door in your home, don't give your cell number out to strangers, and don't ever meet up with a stranger you met in a chat room. *You've Got Mail* is a movie, not reality.

- If you're under sixteen, invest in a whistle to carry with you at all times. When you turn sixteen, talk to your parents about some Mace spray. (I have a cute pink one on my keychain at all times.) You must be sixteen and have a note from your parent allowing you to carry Mace. When you're eighteen, you can look into a Taser. Carrying one may seem pretty scary, but it also may save your life. As with any self-defense weapon, be sure to get training and know how to carry and use it. Talk with your parents about their stance on self-defense weapons and begin to form your own opinions.

- Have a code word with your parents and friends. If you call or text them with the code word, they know you need help. Maybe your code word, "Schnitzel with noodles," simply means, "Mom, come get me from this stupid party."

- Learn self-defense techniques, including how to get out of a wrist grab, choke hold, bear hug (being held from behind), being pinned to the ground, etc. I can't explain how to get out of those; you have to see it. Watch the video for this chapter AND invest in yourself by taking time to watch some awesome videos on YouTube about women's self-defense.

Here are some awesome websites with more tips:

- SelfDefenseforGirls.com
- RooGirl.com
- Voices.yahoo.com/self-defense-tips-every-girl-know
- KidsHealth.org
- TeenAdvice.about.com
- JustYellFire.com

Again, I recommend getting on YouTube and searching "women's self-defense." There are a ton of great videos with glorious knowledge to be learned. There are even videos on how to handle an attacker with a knife or a gun. It's awesomely empowering!

TALES *of* ADVENTURE!

Here's another story about a time when I wish I would have known a few self-defense skills. During the summer after my freshman year of high school, I went to a week-long summer camp with a ton of kids from my school. T'was a fiesta! Toward the end of the week, I was sitting in a circle with a bunch of kids doing a game of some sort when, all of a sudden, I felt a cement bicep wrap tightly around my neck. My "friend"—we shall call him, Mo—thought it would be really funny to choke me.

Maybe I'm just gifted or overly creative, but I can think of a lot of things that could be considered more fun than choking a friend. But that's just me . . . These are the moments when you have to ask yourself, *Is this person really the kind of "friend" I want to hang out with? Maybe I should choose friends with less muscle mass and bigger brains.*

So he's literally choking me. I was pulling on his arm, hitting him with my hands; I even tried scooting back to try to push him off balance. I couldn't breathe. I started seeing stars, and then . . . BLACK! I woke up lying on my back with a bunch of kids staring down at me and a camp leader right in my face yelling at me to wake up. It caused quite a commotion.

When I finally got my wits about me, I looked around for Mo. I found him in a different part of the camp laughing with some other guys. I went up to him and punched him as hard as I could in the arm. "What the crap, Mo? Why did you do that?" I screamed at him, trying to hold back tears.

"Calm down, Jessie, I was just having fun. Lighten up!"

I stared back at him in awe. *Lighten up? Are you kidding me?* He could have seriously hurt me, and to him it was just no big deal. I made sure he learned a lesson by telling the camp leaders how much that freaked me out. Mo got sent home. We didn't hang out again after that. There's nothing wrong with reporting when something serious happens, girls. Reporting dangerous activities is different than being a tattle tale. Talk to a trusted adult when there's a problem in your life. Adults want to help you!

There's also nothing wrong with distancing yourself from "friends" like Mo. You know who I'm talking about. The "friends" that make you feel horrible about yourself or the "friends" that scare you. You can always be kind and tactful, but you don't ever have to continue hanging out with someone who hurts you— emotionally or physically.

I'm happy to say I know exactly how to get out of a choke hold now, thanks to karate—that's valuable stuff.

LEARN KARATE FOR LIFE (LITERALLY)

Some naysayers might tell you that even if you spend a ton of time learning self-defense techniques, you wouldn't actually be able to use them in a real-life situation. They might tell you that when you are in the moment, your heart is racing, that you won't be able to think clearly enough to remember your self-defense training. This is absolutely NOT TRUE!

Sue Wharton is an amazing woman who worked hard to get a black belt in her later years. She says:

With repetitive training of a required skill, the necessary motor units in the muscles are recruited, neurons and synapses are created to control these motor units, and a memory map becomes laid down in the brain which enables the required movement to be evoked quickly and accurately when a stimulus is received. For example, you see a punch coming towards your head (stimulus), and before you know it, you have evaded and blocked it. You didn't think about it; it just seemed to happen automatically! Well, it probably did happen automatically because it's a technique you've practiced over and over again. Your brain just executed the move below your conscious control.[3]

So, if you're in a real-life situation and your adrenaline is pumping, your heart is pounding, and you're totally freaking out, the likelihood of being able to actually defend yourself is so much higher if you have had some self-defense training than if you had no self-defense training at all. Besides, like I said, just having the confidence that self-defense instills can possibly prevent the incident in the first place.

Lisa Raleigh, from the University of Oregon, says:

The empowerment philosophy of self-defense assumes that even when physical defense isn't called for—when women are faced with obnoxious or harassing behavior that may not be imminently dangerous—they can also learn to set clear boundaries.[4]

If a boy is taunting or bugging you in any way, have enough confidence to say, "Stop!" or "Don't touch me!"—even if you don't have to use any self-defense moves. This is how we set boundaries. By having a strong confidence muscle and standing up for yourself with powerful words, you can make it clear that you value yourself.

 **TOOL #9**

Setting Physical Boundaries

WHAT ARE BOUNDARIES?

Boundaries are limits that you set for yourself and others. They can be emotional, physical, spiritual, or mental. It is a line in the sand that you decide on and feel comfortable with. A line that no one is allowed to cross. A boundary should be very specific, that way you don't wonder if it's being crossed. Here are a few examples.

Personal Space Boundary: If someone is looking over your shoulder as you text a friend, turn around and look at them with a quizzical expression. That's all it will take to send the message to give you some space.

Hugging boundary: You could hug someone from the side instead of straight on.

Joking Boundary: If you are around someone who constantly says something rude or obnoxious, followed by a "just kidding," you can let him or her know that you don't like that.

Get the idea?

✏ JOURNAL TIME

Now take a minute and write some boundaries of your own. Fuzzy, feather-topped pens at the ready, please.

_____

_____

_____

_____

_____

_____

_____

_____

_____

_____

_____

_____

_____

_____

SPEAK UP

If someone is getting close to or crossing a boundary, state how you FEEL strongly. If someone is bugging you by hugging you too tightly, or poking you, or even looking at you inappropriately, firmly but calmly say, "I don't like that." Use "I" words when explaining how you feel. First of all, you don't have to ever explain the reason, but if you find yourself in a situation where it would be appropriate, tell the person what makes you feel the way you do. No one can argue with how you feel. "I feel uncomfortable when you do that," is something that no one can fight you on because it is YOUR feeling.

Say "NO!" I know we have already talked about this one, but I'm just going to keep saying it. You can always be kind, tactful, and compassionate, but firmly state it when you feel a boundary being crossed.

JOURNAL TIME

Write some phrases, and practice them in the mirror so you don't have to think about what to say if that boundary is crossed.

_____

_____

_____

BENEFITS OF SELF-DEFENSE TRAINING

Here are some of the benefits of learning self-defense and/or getting a black belt in some form of martial arts:

- You learn how to defend your body if you were ever in a violent situation.

- You feel empowered and confident because you know you carry this valuable knowledge.

- Everyone at school thinks you're freaking awesome because they know you could kick their trash.

- Your family and friends respect you.

- You respect yourself.

- You learn to be disciplined.

- You gain a great work ethic.

- You are much less of a target for a predator simply because of the way you carry yourself. (Again, it's a fact that predators look for girls who come across as weak and timid. They look for girls who they think won't fight back.)

- You learn self-control. Controlling your strength is vital in karate.

- You set a priceless example for the girls around you. You become a leader.

The most important statistic that supports my belief of the importance of self-defense comes from a study by the Department of Justice and the Centers for Disease Control and Prevention. This study found that one in six women reported being assaulted, and 52 percent of these assaults occurred with girls under the age of eighteen.[5] These are frightening facts that should really make you think about how you would handle a situation where you may have to fight for your life.

Please remember, you are worth protecting!

 GO AHEAD AND *FEED THE BEAR*, YOU DARLING, *DASHBOARD PUPPY.* 9ER OVER . . .

CONFIDENT, CLASSY LADIES VALUE THEMSELVES ENOUGH TO PROTECT THEIR BODIES.

 CHALLENGE

Choose to value your safety enough to try a self-defense class and see how you feel about the whole shebang ... I'll bet my tapioca pudding you feel amazingly empowered after just one punch to a punching bag! Try a class. It might even be free to try it one time—ask when you call.

... it all comes down to our choices.

WRITE ABOUT YOUR EXPERIENCE:

_____

_____

_____

_____

_____

_____

_____

_____

_____

_____

_____

SOCIAL & DINING ETIQUETTE

O kay, before you roll your eyes and start turning the page to skip this chapter, STOP! I know the word *etiquette* is really old fashioned and boring, but if you've never discussed it before, then I promise it's not what you think. We are not going to spend the next few pages talking about doilies and crossing our ankles. I'll spend 7.5 percent of this chapter talking about which fork to use at a fancy-shmancy restaurant. The most important lesson here is about social etiquette.

If you look up *etiquette* in the dictionary you'll find something like this: "the rules indicating the proper and polite way to behave."[1]

MY defintition of etiquette is making people around you feel comfortable.

Helping people feel comfortable is a good thing and very worthwhile to learn. You wouldn't have even cracked this book open if you weren't interested in leading a great life. Being aware of others is an easy way to feed your happiness and confidence. Learning how to be a graceful, classy lady is a skill that will benefit your life and the lives of those around you. People love to be around someone who genuinely cares about THEIR comfort!

When I first told my family that I wanted to teach dining etiquette to teenage girls, every single one of them buck snorted as they threw their heads back and chortled!

If you knew me growing up, you would also laugh at the absurdity that I am teaching this skill now! I promise I don't teach it because I am such an expert or I am such a refined, classy woman. I teach it because I wish I had been taught, and because SOMEONE needs to teach it! In my teen years, with two masculine brothers and a hammer-swinging, mountain-climbing, scouting-extraordinaire father, I was able to be very casual about my table manners, which I loved. I am very real and casual. I would never expect myself or anyone else to behave like the Queen of England at all times: always sitting at a table with ankles crossed, napkin in lap, wearing crisp white gloves, taking teeny-tiny bites of each piece of meat. That is just not realistic. I know exactly how it is to be starving and only having two minutes to eat your lunch, so the only option is to inhale your food right out of the refrigerator. Believe me, I get what real life looks like.

Learning dining etiquette skills is really only for times when you are in a very formal setting, and you find yourself looking at your place setting wondering which fork to use.

As I said, the whole point of social and dining etiquette is to make everyone around you feel comfortable. You want your friends and family to feel relaxed and calm in your presence. YOU want to feel confident and relaxed, as well. That is what these 12 Skills of Ladyhood are all about . . . confidence.

Here's a mortifying story for you . . .

👢 TALES *of* ADVENTURE!

One night, when my husband and I were dating, we were dining at a fancy-shmancy restaurant, and half-way through our meal, he worked up his courage and said, "Jessie, I don't know if you want to know this, but if it were me, I would want to know." He continued to politely inform me that I chew with my mouth open. Talk about wanting to crawl under a table and die! I considered never dating him ever again because I was so embarrassed to be me. But, I'm so glad he had the courage to tell me because I honestly did not know. I had grown up doing pageants and other ladylike activities, but somewhere in my teenage years, I stopped paying attention to my manners and began creating bad habits.

Sometimes we need people in our lives to be brave enough to tell us things they know we would want to improve in ourselves. Take that kind of stuff with a grain of salt, but be open-minded because we can learn so much from other people. Wouldn't you rather be aware that your zipper is down or you have food in your teeth? I know I would! Don't let your pride or your ego get in the way of something that can really help you live a great life.

Sometimes the truth hurts but it's exactly what we need.

Psychologist John Rosemond perfectly sums up what I'm saying: "Manners and respect are inseparable. [I] believe children can never learn to respect themselves unless they learn respect for others."[2]

DINING ETIQUITTE 101

Since we humans have to eat food every day of our lives, we might as well learn to do it right! Here we go with dining etiquette 101!

As I've said, formal dining etiquette is really only for when you're out at a fancy restaurant. Maybe you're interviewing for a job, or you're out with a really gorgeous guy, or maybe you're out with your gorgeous guy's parents! Whatever the situation, you want to have enough emotional intelligence to turn on the "manners switch" and put on your best behavior. This is where confidence comes in. Dining etiquette requires us to have confidence to behave in a classy way, and it also gives us confidence when we know exactly what appropriate behavior is in the first place.

 **TOOL #10**

DINING WITH CONFIDENCE

1   When in doubt, start from the outside and work in. Use the outermost fork for the salad or appetizer, the

outermost spoon for the first course or soup, the inner fork or spoon for the main course.

2   Place your napkin on your lap while eating, on the table if you have to leave, but never on your chair.

3   Use the community butter knife to get a slice of butter on your plate, then use your own knife to spread it onto your bread.

4   Dessert utensils are always at the top of your plate.

5   Slow down and take small bites, enjoy your food, and give your body a little help in digestion.

6   Wait until everyone at your table has their food before you begin eating.

7   Pass the salt and pepper together, even if someone only asks for one.

8   Don't reach past your placemat. If you need something, ask someone to pass it to you.

9   Don't blow your nose, chew with your mouth open, scratch your skin, or put on makeup at the table.

10   Don't ever use your cloth napkin to wipe your face or your nose. Use it only to dab at your mouth or cover your mouth while chewing.

Fiona Cameron Williams from the FCW Hospitality in New York says, "Learning proper dining etiquette as a teenager sets the stage for future interviews, social events and internships teens will experience in a few years."[3]

Having good table manners will not only impress your future boss or college professor, it will also impress your friends, the guys you date, and basically everyone around you! Leaders have good manners.

AND NOW, ON TO . . . SOCIAL ETIQUETTE

Before we get into the do's and don'ts of social interaction, I want to mention one aspect of social etiquette that I care a lot about—clothing. Let me illustrate why . . .

TALES *of* ADVENTURE!

When I was a freshman in high school, my older brother was a senior, and I just thought he was the coolest guy on the planet. He was and still is a role model to me. He was nice enough and patient enough to let me hang out with his senior friends. I really enjoyed his friends because they were very nice to me, and they were also really cute!

One day, I was hanging out with one of his friends during lunch, and I was wearing a pretty short skirt that I thought was adorable at the time. Trying to be flirtatious, I sat on his lap. I didn't think anything of it because I just thought I was being cute and fun. My brother told me later that I had made his friend very uncomfortable. I had no idea, and I felt so embarrassed about it!

This was such a good lesson about the power of what we wear and how our wardrobe can affect boys—and all humans for that matter. Important note: even though etiquette is about making other people comfortable around us, I would never encourage you to only dress to please others. Your clothing choices should reflect your fabulous individual style and your own modesty boundaries.

WHAT IS IN YOUR CLOSET?

Here's the part where I will never tell you what you should or shouldn't wear. It's not my place. Exact measurements on your hemline is a personal decision for you to make and feel good about.

I am not afraid, however, to share my personal standards of modesty with you. Feel free to disagree. Decide where you stand. Jessie's personal modesty boundaries are . . . no cleavage, no midriff, and no miniskirts.

I also care a lot about what my daughter wears. Because of that, I want to be a great example and always go above and beyond (think about our leadership chat in Skill #2). I choose to behave above reproach because I want to be a leader and I want to be a person of character. I am so far from perfect, but just wanting to be our best is a great place to start.

It is my personal view that keeping yourself clothed and modest only makes you more attractive, more elegant, and yes, even sexier. Yep, I said it. Sexiness isn't the most important thing, of course, but it is a very natural desire for women, and we don't have to hide that—we just have to find the balance. It would be unhealthy for you to not acknowledge that desire in yourself.

Your modesty boundaries might be different than mine—stricter or more relaxed, and that's okay. You might have different opinions than your parents or guardians, and that's okay, too. They definitely get to have a say; it's their job, and if they are strict about what you wear, don't get mad at them. We need parents who are brave enough to fight for virtue and classiness. It is very important to respect your house rules. When you become an adult, what will YOUR personal standards be? We all get to make personal choices. My goal here is just to help you think about the choices you make and whether or not those choices make those around you comfortable. Again, that is what etiquette is all about.

So many of our celebrities who reveal as much skin as possible leaving nothing to the imagination are sending a pretty clear message that they want attention. It could be possible that they don't value themselves enough to want the attention focused in other, more important, areas of their lives such as intellect, service, ambition, soul, talents, or personality. This could be up for debate, but think about how you feel about what our media portrays as sleek, modern, and sexy. Where should our attention be focused?

Start developing your own ideas and setting your own boundaries. Talk to your parents about it. Ask them why they feel the way they do about what you wear, and then share how you feel about it. Just remember that if you want them to listen to you, make the effort to really listen to them, as well. Maybe if you make it an open, honest conversation, you might be able to avoid arguing every morning over what you're wearing as you head off to school. 😊

My husband often tells me that he thinks I am sexier when I'm covered up because he loves my classiness. I love hearing that. He values my mind, my heart, my femininity, and elegance more than my skin and body. More importantly, I want the way I dress to show the world that I am confident and that I see my own value. That is what I hope for you. That is what I hope for my own daughter.

What is the message your clothes send? Are you communicating sophistication, maturity, classiness, elegance, and confidence, or like some of our celebrities, are you non-verbally screaming that you need attention and are insecure. I am here to say that it is very possible to be sexy without being revealing. There is a huge difference. It's very possible to be stunning, cute, sassy, and fun while also being classy.

Classiness isn't just about what you wear or how you eat, though; it's about how you carry yourself. What are you communicating? Here are other areas of social etiquette that are very important to think about.

 **TOOL #11**

Social Etiquette Rock Stars!

1   **Including Friends:** How hard is it to include others? If you're standing in a circle chatting with friends and

someone else walks up, take a step back, open up the circle, put your arm around her, and say, "Hey, we were just talking about the glorious aroma of Cheetos. Join us!" Not hard. Include everyone. Be a leader!

2   **Gossip:** "If you can't say anything nice, at least have the decency to be vague."—Susan Andersen. There is a difference between venting and gossiping. If you need advice on how to handle a sticky situation with one of your friends, vent to a trusted adult—not one of your other friends. That's just gossiping. Get the negative emotions out because that's very healthy and important, but once they're out, move on! If you're still having a hard time with the friend, talk to her face-to-face and try to solve the problem head-on. That's an awesome way to exercise your leadership muscle.

3   **Rumors:** If you've ever had a rumor spread about you, you know how much this hurts. Don't spread poison.

4   **Cell Phone Manners:** We could just call this technology manners. Sometimes we have to unplug and connect with humans in the old-fashioned way. Don't chat on your cell while going through the checkout at the store, don't have deeply personal cell chats when you're in public, and—pay attention to this one—do not text while driving!

5   **Eye Contact:** People think you do not care about them if you don't look them in the eye while they're talking. Make eye contact.

6   **Listening Skills:** I'm sure you hate it when you're interrupted. (It's my biggest pet peeve!) When we are engaged and present with our friends and family by listening skillfully, we show respect.

7   **Respect:** Have respect for parents, teachers, administrators, friends, and gentlemen. Basically, respect everyone.

8   **Emotional Intelligence:** Know when it's appropriate to be wild and crazy and when it's appropriate to be calm and collected.

9   **Socially Uncomfortable Situations:** We all have to face these—how to dump a boyfriend, how to tell your best friend that her drama is really bugging you, how to say no to a friend's invitation to go to a party you know will be alcohol-ridden and uncomfortable for you, how to handle that one crazy aunt of yours at family reunions who still treats you like you're four, how to manage when you see an old friend and forget their name . . . each situation is different. A good rule of thumb is be honest by stating the problem clearly and how you FEEL about it. No one can ever argue with how you feel. In the case of forgetting someone's name, just call it out—be honest. The secret to handling most uncomfortable situations is really just to be honest and use humor. It's so much better to laugh and call it out than to try to skirt around the issue.

10 **Dating Etiquette:** This is a big one because you know how I feel about girls allowing guys to behave like gentlemen. Lisa Grotts from *Seventeen Magazine* answers the question: "Should a girl expect her date to hold the door for her or give her his jacket when she's cold? Are these expectations outdated?"

Lisa's reply: "Everything above is still in style and forever will be. There is no distinction between men and women when it comes to social graces. Girls should expect that their date will behave this way—if they don't, they need to learn how!"[4]

11 **"Just kidding:"** Do you have a friend who says mean, obnoxious things and dismisses it by ending the sentence with " . . . just kidding"? Saying these words does not excuse cruel words.

When we make a conscious choice to be respectful toward other humans—and we back that choice up with a lot of real effort—our confidence level shoots through the roof! It's a huge win-win.

It is the natural human experience to have awkward moments. Let's embrace them and learn to laugh about them. So, purely for entertainment purposes, here are some awesomely embarrassing moments that we can all relate to . . .

- You check your phone because you have nothing to contribute to the conversation.

- You wait for the right time to say something; you get interrupted. Twice.

- Someone you vaguely know is walking in front of you. You maintain distance.

- You hold the door for someone. They're slightly too far away.

- Someone comes online, and you say, "Hey." They go offline.

- You go in for the high-five. The other person isn't looking.

- You accidentally look someone in the eye. You pretend to look past them.

- You say something stupid. You play it down, but everyone sees your face going red.

- You say, "Hi!" to someone. It comes out as a whisper.

- Your friends formed a circle while you were gone. You can't fit in and end up standing slightly askew. (Remember how to include, so you don't let this happen to someone else.)

- Waiting by yourself for friends, you pretend you're texting.

- You tell a hilarious joke. Nobody laughs.

- The girl cutting your hair talks to the hairstylist next to you. You respond.

- Walking down the hallway, you make eye contact too early.

- Someone goes in for the high-five. You accidentally hug them.

- You're introducing someone to a group of people. You forget their name.

- You're introducing someone to a group of people. You say the wrong name.

- Friend: "Hi" . . . . . . You: "Good thanks."

- You eavesdrop on a stranger's conversation. You laugh out loud at the funny part.

- You decide to wear your awesome new jacket. You see a girl wearing the exact same one.

Don't beat yourself up when you have embarrassing moments . . . just laugh! Look out and be ready to lend a hand to a friend—or total stranger—if you see they are having one of those moments. Confidence boost!

The lost art of Ladyhood
can be reclaimed if we can
CHOOSE to be a generation
of fabulous ladies who are
respectful enough to care
about the comfort of the
people around us.

CHALLENGE

Try making your family or friends or your boyfriend (awwww!) . . . a glorious meal! Set the table all fancy and serve them like a French waiter—accent optional. At least it will make for something fun to do that's out of the ordinary. Let's be honest, you can only play Minecraft for so long before you want to put shards of glass in your eye. Do something different! Teach dining etiquette to your favorite people! Choose to have manners . . . it all comes down to our choices.

WRITE ABOUT YOUR EXPERIENCE:

_____

_____

_____

_____

_____

_____

_____

_____

SERVICE

"IF YOU CAN'T FEED A HUNDRED PEOPLE,

THEN JUST FEED ONE."

—MOTHER TERESA

I'm going to say something really mean. Ready? Teenagers are selfish. I know I sure was! I know that sounds cruel, but actually it's just part of our natural development. You already know how much I love you, so this fact is said with nothing but adoration for you.

YOU *ADORABLE GUM BALL MACHINE!*

In general, the teen years are very self-centered years of anyone's life. As children and teens, we humans are naturally this way, and it's not necessarily a bad thing. We are trying to figure out this crazy life. We are born into this world and instantly discover we don't get a ton of choices. As babies, we don't choose our parents, our names, our homes, our food . . . as kids, we don't choose our school, where we sit in our classrooms, what's for dinner, when we get days off . . . and as teens, we don't get to choose homework assignments, learning disorders, acne, drama in our social lives, height, or even the shape of our ears.

On the flip side, there are plenty of things we do have a say in: our attitude, our dreams, our work ethic, anger, forgiveness, character, honesty, and—here's a biggie—our happiness!

It's important to realize that the "selfish switch" can be turned on and off. We need to have enough emotional intelligence to know when it's okay to think about ourselves and when it's important to think about others.

It is so important to learn how to control that switch, because when we are able to take the focus off ourselves for a minute and think about someone else, we become better people. When we take time to serve others, we become happier. This is a scientific fact: if you want to be happier, do something nice for someone else. You probably already know how good it feels to make someone smile or to know you truly helped someone, but in case you don't know, it's like a drug. You want an awesome, non-life-threatening way to get high? Go out of your way to make someone smile, and you will feel awesome about your life.

Serving someone doesn't have to be complicated or take a ton of time. Simply smiling at someone in the hall; writing your mom a quick thank-you note; telling your math teacher, "Thank you for teaching me"; sharing a candy bar with your younger brother; helping your elderly neighbor by mowing his lawn; or inviting that lonely kid to sit at your group's table at lunch are all very simple things that will seriously make you feel like a rock star! It will shock you how good it feels. Of course, the people you serve will totally love you forever, but the benefit YOU get when you make an effort to share your light with the humans around you is a powerful lift all by its onesie.

Check out this awesome girl who is CHOOSING to share her light and serve others.

Alisha King began volunteering at age fifteen, leading her to start and become CEO of her own organization: UniConnect. She says, "[By] learning from people who are from all walks of life and have had different opportunities and knock-backs, [I gain] self-worth. I feel like I'm making a positive difference to society. I feel like my life has meaning and direction."[1]

I want to take a second to chat about something you might not think would fit into a chapter on service . . . depression. So many young ladies suffer from this. I know I sure did at different times during my teen years, and it can be crippling. This is an important topic because I want you to know that almost all humans feel depressed at different times in their lives. According to the National Institute of Mental Health, girls are more likely to struggle with depression than boys, and 11 percent of adolescents develop a depressive disorder by age eighteen.[2] If you struggle with depression, service can be an incredibly powerful form of therapy. Now, I'm not saying service can or should take the place of medications and therapies that doctors will suggest; I'm just saying that it can DEFINITELY help as an additional boost.

How do you know if you are depressed? Here are some symptoms of depression from helpguide.org. If you have two or more, it's ALWAYS a good idea to talk to someone about it. There is never, ever, ever any shame in going to see a professional therapist or talking to your doctor. There is help for this condition. You do not just have to "tough it out."

- You constantly feel irritable or angry.

- Nothing seems fun anymore, and you just don't see the point of trying.

- You feel bad about yourself—worthless, guilty, or just "wrong" in some way.

- You sleep too much or not enough.

- You have frequent unexplained headaches or other physical problems.

- Anything and everything makes you cry.

- You've gained or lost weight without consciously trying to.

- You just can't concentrate. Your grades may be plummeting because of it.

- You feel helpless and hopeless.

- You are thinking of death or suicide. If this is true talk to someone NOW.[3]

Is your friend depressed? You might just be their guardian angel and their lifeline by looking for these warning signs.

- Your friend doesn't want to do the things you guys used to love to do.
- Your friend starts using alcohol or drugs or hanging with a bad crowd.
- Your friend stops going to classes and afterschool activities.
- Your friend talks about being bad, ugly, stupid, or worthless.
- Your friend starts talking about death or suicide.[4]

Noticing these symptoms is just one side of this coin. Do something about it! Talk to your friend and tell them that there is ALWAYS hope and a light at the end of the tunnel. Kids who attempt suicide usually say they did it because they felt there was absolutely no other option to solve their problems.

If you or anyone you know has thoughts of suicide, call this number: 1-800-273-TALK. There is always hope and help!

If you struggle with depression or even if you're a basically happy person who just wants to feel more fulfillment and a stronger sense of purpose, service can be just what the doctor ordered!

On livescience.com, Michael Steger, a psychologist at the University of Louisville in Kentucky, says that he has always been amazed by how differently people lead their lives. He says,

"Pat Tillman, for example, left the NFL to enlist in the Army and fight in Iraq and later Afghanistan (where he was killed), but celebrity and socialite Paris Hilton continually pursues a public life of shallowness."[5]

Because of this observation, Steger did a study with 65 undergraduate students with the goal being to find out what makes people happier—seeking pleasure or doing good? "We found that the more people participated in meaningful activities, the happier they were and the more purposeful their lives felt. Pleasure-seeking behaviors, on the other hand, did not make people happier."[6]

In another study from *Healthy Living*, we learn that the idea of helping others to help yourself is finding a lot of traction in the scientific community:

New research suggests there may be a biochemical explanation for the positive emotions associated with doing good. In a recent study published in the *Proceedings of the National Academy of Science*, participants' brains were monitored by MRI scans while they made decisions about donating part of their research payment to charitable organizations. When participants chose to donate money, the brain's mesolimbic system was activated, the same part of the brain that's activated in response to monetary rewards and other positive stimuli. Choosing to donate also activated the brain's subgenual area, the part of the brain that produces feel-good chemicals, like oxytocin, that promote social bonding.[7]

That's a mouthful, but it makes perfect sense. We are BUILT to get happy from helping others!

In the same article, Stephen Post, PhD, a research professor of bioethics at Case Western Reserve University who co-authored the book *Why Good Things Happen to Good People* says, "When you're experiencing compassion, benevolence, and kindness, they push aside the negative emotions. One of the best ways to overcome stress is to do something to help someone else."[8]

The article goes on to say, "Since depression, anxiety, and stress involve a high degree of focus on the self, focusing on the needs of others literally helps shift our thinking."[9]

Those are some pretty convincing arguments, I'd say.

 DO YOU CONCUR, *CHECKPOINT CHARLIE?* I KNEW YOU WOULD.

TALES *of* ADVENTURE!

When I was eighteen, my life changed forever. I went to Kenya, Africa, with a service organization called Reach the Children. (That's ReachTheChildren.org for your web-surfing pleasure.) I remember being on the twenty-two-hour plane ride thinking, *I'm so excited to get there! Those poor people, life must be so hard for them. They don't have all the wonderful things we have in America. I'm so glad we can help them!* I was genuinely excited and motivated to improve their educational conditions, but I was so naïve in my attitude of how those people lived. That's why the experience changed my life forever.

When our team arrived in Nairobi, I was stunned at what a thriving city it was! I thought all of Africa was primitive and destitute. But when we traveled just outside the city, a very different picture was painted, and my transformation began. Out of nowhere came beautiful little children, running around on the dirt roads with no shoes and ragged clothes. The houses were made out of corrugated metal sheets duct taped together, and you could see what they considered a sewer system, running openly along the side of the road. It was all they knew. My heart was torn, and the scene overwhelmed me.

We made our way to an orphanage, where the children had prepared a performance for us. There were at least a hundred kids of all ages, and they put on an incredible show. They sang and danced and did acrobatic tricks—I was so impressed with their beautiful talents. If any of these kids had tried out for *America's Got Talent* or *American Idol*, they'd have stolen the show, no question about it. We spent a couple of hours hanging out with these amazing young people, sharing crackers, learning their songs, and taking pictures with them. These children had absolutely nothing, and yet they were so happy and grateful for life. I soaked it up. It was marvelous!

From the orphanage, we drove to a little school Reach the Children had built. All the kids were in matching red uniforms, had nutritious food, and were learning how to read and write. I spent time with a group of young boys who were *obsessed* with my video camera. They would line up to take turns looking through the lens. We played Red Light, Green Light and Down by the Banks and had a blast! The next day, we were on our way to another school in a little city called Molo. It was out in the middle of nowhere. There were no paved roads; in fact, the potholes were more like craters, and apparently Africa is short on shock absorbers—we had to hold on for dear life as we bounced down the road! All the people we saw were wearing filthy, ripped clothing, and there was no deodorant—the smell was sometimes overpowering. At one point, we stopped at a rest stop to use the bathroom and were completely shocked to discover what they used for toilets—open stalls with no doors—just a little hole in the ground. No flusher, nowhere to sit—quite a shock!

One of my favorite experiences in Africa was arriving at the school in Molo and having a horde of beautiful kids sprint over to hug us. They didn't know us, but they were so happy to have us visit that they flipped out when we got out of our van. They would look at the freckles on my arm and try to scratch them off—they rarely saw white people. A lot of these babes were orphans, and, in their short lives, most of them had already experienced extreme starvation, homelessness, and the death of their parents. Some had become thieves before they came to this school, as stealing food was the only way they could survive. And yet, they were such happy humans.

The main purpose for our visit was to build these kids a library. We brought hundreds of books for them. We spent hours organizing their new library, cataloging books, and—my favorite—reading to the kids. They would jump up on my lap and say, "Read this one." Then after I read it, they'd hop down, grab another book, and jump back into my lap and say, "Read this one, too!" I was inspired by their enthusiasm for education. Some of these sweet children hadn't ever had the opportunity to learn before they came to this school . . . and they were so grateful.

I tell you all of this to give you a feel for why my life was transformed. You can't have experiences such as these without being touched deeply. But the greatest impact on my heart was made by a sparkling thirteen-year-old African girl named Cindy. I adored this spunky, sweet lady instantly! She had a dazzling smile, glittering eyes, and gorgeous black skin. She was so stunning, and her happiness was contagious. We spent an entire day together, reading to younger kids, hiking up a small mountain behind the school, painting walls, and playing games.

The whole day she was telling me about how she was so grateful for this school, and that she was going to work so hard to graduate. She wanted to become a psychologist when she grew up. She even told me about her office she had designed in her head.

She painted an exciting picture for me: "I'm going to have a cherry wood desk, and it will always be clean. There won't ever be any papers on it. And I want to have a cream-colored chaise lounge chair so that when people come into my office they will be so comfortable. And on my walls I want a lovely, ornate gray-colored wallpaper that will be so classy. When people come into my office, they will feel safe, and I will be able to help them with their problems."

Here is a girl who has dreamed her dream, right? Can you visualize her spectacular office right now? She was so excited about this goal, and nothing was going to stop her.

The next day, I had to say goodbye to Cindy. We were headed to another school. We promised we would write to each other and stay in touch. On the bus ride to the next school, my team leader came and sat by me, "How was your day yesterday?"

"It was fantastic! I made a new friend named Cindy, and we had a blast together! We're even going to be pen pals!"

He was silent for a second, and then he asked, "Did she tell you about herself?" I went into all the exciting details Cindy had given me about her goals for the future. "That's neat, but did she tell you about her childhood?"

I paused. "No, she didn't."

He smiled politely, "Well, if you're going to be pen pals, you probably need to know a little more about her."

He went on to explain to me that Cindy's father had abandoned her mother when she was very young, and then her mother had died from AIDS. She was taken in by some distant relatives who did not want her, and she was forced to sleep in a cardboard box outside their hut. There was a lot of physical and emotional abuse in that home. He also said that Cindy was living at the school since it was too dangerous for her to walk there from her house.

Reach the Children had built a boarding house at this school for the safety of the older girls like Cindy. When my team leader explained the danger these girls faced as they walked miles and miles to and from school, I cried my eyes out. It's a little harsh to hear, but I'm going to share it with you, darling reader, because I know you can be mature enough to handle it and because there is such an important lesson in it. You see, in Africa, some people believe that when a man has AIDS, he can rid himself of it by raping a virgin. Of course, this only spreads the disease further. Cindy had already been attacked and raped, and she was only thirteen years old and now had to deal with being HIV positive. Talk about not having choices! Can you imagine how hard that would be?

I cried for a long time, my heart breaking for my sweet friend, but then I realized something incredible. Never once did she tell me that her life was hard because she was an orphan. Never once did she complain about being abandoned by her father. Never once did she mention that she was a victim of rape and abuse. This is a girl who owned her life! She had chosen to have the strength to move on from the past, to be happy in the present, and to focus on her hope-filled future.

I will never forget Cindy. Whenever I feel sorry for myself, or I want to complain about my life, I think of her. I think of how grateful she would be to have even one tenth of the things I have—indoor plumbing, safe and plentiful food, microwaves, automobiles, shoes, showers, clean water, education and knowledge at my fingertips, clean clothing, and the blessing of walking down the street and feeling safe. So, the next time we want to whine about our world, let's remember Cindy's world, and CHOOSE to be grateful.

This story sums up what I'm trying to teach you about service. Here I was thinking I was going to serve these beautiful African people when it was ME who was served. They taught me so much and blessed my life in more ways than I can describe to you—service is a win-win!

What are some simple things you can do to help someone else? Here are some ideas to get you thinking.

 ## TOOL #12

Serve Someone

- Smile at that shy kid in your English class.

- Visit an animal shelter and give some sweet dogs and cats some love.

- Write your best friend a "You're awesome!" note.

- Say "Hi" to someone new every day.

- Write an anonymous "You're awesome!" note to that lonely girl in your science class. Drop it in her locker or onto her desk when she's not looking.

- Invite that one kid who always sits by himself to sit with your friends at lunch so he doesn't have to be alone again.

- Help your widowed neighbor plant flowers in her garden.

- Write your parents a "Thanks for loving me and not putting me up for adoption" note and leave it under their pillow.

- Take your little sister to a movie.

- Make cookies for your mailman with a thank-you note, and leave it on top or inside your mailbox.

- Make cookies for your garbage man with a big poster that says "Thank you, garbage man!" (I actually asked my garbage man what they like to be called and he said they don't care if they're called "garbage men.")

- Make cookies for your school janitor.

- Make cookies for your principal. Shameless brown-nosing never hurt anyone. ☺

- Get a group of friends to go to a nursing home and paint all the ladies' nails.

- Find creative ways to thank firemen, policemen, doctors, and nurses for putting their lives on the line every day for us.

- Make dinner for your parents.

- Here's a doozy . . . do something nice for your school bully or someone that you really don't like. The outcome just might be amazing. Sometimes bullies need the most love.

- If you notice something cool about someone, tell them: "I like your shirt," "Nice shoes," or "You have glorious ear lobes."

- Organize fundraisers, bake sales, and yard sales, or even door-to-door selling of homemade items. The funds can go to your favorite local charity. To discover a charity you'd like to support, Google "service projects."

- Teach or tutor—what are your skills? Are you good at reading and writing? Can you visit an elementary school and take some time with a child that needs a little one-on-one attention? Maybe you are a wonderful dancer. You can start a free community dance class. So many kids want to be involved in the arts, but can't afford it. You might be an answer to a prayer for that child.

- Volunteer at homeless shelters or soup kitchens—any homeless shelter would flip out to have your help serving people in need. Google "homeless shelter" and specify your area to find the closest one to you.

Service will help YOU! It certainly helps those that you serve, but the emotional benefits YOU get far outweigh what you give. If you feel down, dark, heavy, bored, or full-on depressed, get outside yourself and think of someone else. It will feel so good . . . you'll want the feeling all the time.

Wanna be happy? Service is a sure-fire tool to help you get there.

✐ JOURNAL TIME

You don't have to travel to Africa to serve someone. Jot down your ideas. Where is your cheetah-print pen?

_____

_____

_____

Your turn . . . think! What are your talents? What are the needs you see around you?

_____

_____

_____

If you had a million dollars and had to give it away, what charity or cause would you help? Pet shelters? AIDS? Heart disease? Kids with cancer? Or you might even start your own charity! What do you think? What cause could you, or do you, feel passionate about?

_____

_____

_____

Think of a time someone served you and made your day.

_____

_____

_____

IF WE CAN LEARN TO STEP OUTSIDE OURSELVES TO HELP OTHER PEOPLE, WE WILL BE WELL ON OUR WAY TO RECLAIMING THAT LOST ART OF LADYHOOD.

 CHALLENGE

Choose to do something nice for someone else once a day this week. You can spend all of five seconds on a smile to a shy kid in the hall or do something more elaborate. See how you feel at the end of the week. If you're not feeling even slightly happy or proud of yourself, email me, and I'll mail you a pony . . . that's how much I'm willing to wager that you will feel awesome after seven acts of pure kindness towards others.

. . . it all comes down to our choices.

WRITE ABOUT YOUR EXPERIENCE:

_____

_____

_____

_____

_____

_____

_____

_____

_____

SKILL #7

HEALTH

"Fitness to me is not about a crunch or a pushup, it's about taking your power back."

—JILLIAN MICHAELS

I f you don't have your health, you don't have anything. You've heard it a million times, and it's true. If you've ever had any health challenge, you know it is true. If you've watched someone close to you go through health challenges . . . you know it's true. Your health is such an important element to a happy life, and it's something you can choose to cherish.

Take care of your body. Be gentle with yourself. Be kind to yourself. Think of your body as a totally different person than you. "You" are your mind, personality, and soul. Your body is the glove that you live in. Having this perspective can help you appreciate your health.

Let's think about all the fantastical things our bodies can do.

- Can you bend your fingers, your knees, your elbows? Do all your joints work?

- Can you see sunsets?

- Are your ear lobes symmetrical? Seriously though, do you have ear lobes?

- When you cut your finger, does it heal?

- Does it hurt when you walk, or do you live basically pain free?

- Are you physically able to smell the glorious aroma of chimichangas?

- Are you able to add 2 + 2 in your head? So, your brain works?

- Can you listen to your favorite song on the radio?

- Can you feel heat and cold?

- Are you physically able to taste your mom's mouthwatering turnip soup?

If you answered yes to even two of these questions, you have a body to be thankful for. Appreciate your body for all the absolutely miraculous things it does. Don't focus on the things it doesn't do.

Now that we've established that you have an incredible, glorious, magical physical body, let's chat about some ways you can create good habits for taking care of it.

EXERCISE AND NUTRITION

Yep, you knew I was going to say it. There is no way around it. There is work that must be done to have a healthy life. There is just no way to opt out of exercise and eating right.

 WE ARE ALL ON THIS TRAIN TOGETHER *PAPER HANGER!* ☺

I care a lot about this because when I was a teen and was struggling with the pressures of teen-life, I made a very hazardous choice to not respect my health. I chose to deal with my insecurities through bulimia. I chose to hurt my body and my singing voice because I didn't cherish or understand the gift of my health enough. It makes me sad to think about that choice I made, and I try to make up for it every day by being kind to my skin, my eyes, my hair, my toes, and my heart. I am so thankful for how good my body has been to me, and now, I choose to cherish it. Think about what your body has done for you, and focus on those good things. I promise if you make a conscious decision to see the good things, you will start feeling happier about the body you live in. ☺

EXERCISE FOR BODY AND MIND

It's important to know that not all the benefits are physical. There are awesome MENTAL benefits, too! Dr. Allison Williams of The American College of Sports Medicine tells us, "Adolescents can also reap numerous mental health benefits from physical activity, especially as it relates to depression. A 2006 study showed higher levels of sport participation and physical activity were linked to lower levels of depression, and that exercise can encourage better self-perception. This is very important for teen girls."[1]

Whenever I'm having a down day and all I want to do is stay in bed with a plate full of Easy Mac watching *Harry Potter*, I try to give myself a small task to do. Instead of doing a full workout, I make it more achievable and not so overwhelming. A walk around the block, do one hundred jumping jacks, take ten deep breaths, spend fifteen minutes on the elliptical . . . a bite-size workout instead of the full enchilada on "those days." It's amazing what happens! When I'm done with my mini workout, I feel better. I have more energy, and I'm ready to conquer the day. I have experienced the connection between exercise and our state of mind—it is real.

Okay let's start being productive and chat about how we can be healthy and happy.

TOOL #13

Love Your Body

What is your favorite form of physical activity? If you create an exercise plan that involves something you already love, you'll be more successful in maintaining consistency. Do you love:

- Running
- Hiking
- Swimming
- Biking
- Pogo stick jumping (Seriously, it's a great workout!)
- Lifting weights
- Yoga
- Sports
- Dancing

Any and all of these are great ways to get your heart pumping and give your body the push it needs to keep you strong.

✏ JOURNAL TIME

Go find your smiley face pencil. What are your favorite ways to be active?

_____

_____

_____

_____

_____

Scientific research has found a whole slew of fabulous random facts about exercise. I love random facts! Check these out:

- People who exercise as little as fifteen minutes a day have a 14 percent lower mortality risk than people who don't exercise at all.

- Exercisers can improve their performance by as much as 50 percent if they eat dark chocolate regularly.

- Depressed people can alleviate their symptoms by as much as 47 percent with regular aerobic exercise.

- Three times as many college graduates as high-school dropouts exercise regularly.

- Exercisers can improve their performance by as much as 15 percent if they listen to music while working out.

- Avid swimmers have a 50 percent lower mortality rate than runners, walkers, and people who don't exercise at all.

- Teens who exercise are 36 percent less likely to develop brain tumors than teens who don't.[2]

I would never claim to be a health expert, but from my own experience, I want to tell you that I have learned to LOVE exercise.

TALES of ADVENTURE!

I used to hate, hate, hate running. In college, I just about died of boredom and from my lungs exploding while running one mile in my fitness class. But then I learned how good running is for your lungs, and since I'm a singer, I was very interested. I started with just ten minutes a day, literally, just going around my block. I absolutely hated every second, but I pushed myself and kept going, increasing the time I would spend by a minute or two each week. It took about three months, but I eventually got up to three miles a day, and—the surprise of my life—I was actually excited to get my running shoes on every morning. It may seem weird, but those endorphins are totally real and awesome!

Exercise can help you feel happy—I have experienced it first-hand. So, maybe you have to push yourself to get started, but I promise you will find the groove, and it will feel so good that you will want to do it every day. The hardest part is starting. Whether you start with something you love or something you loathe . . . just start! Even ten minutes a day getting your heart pumping is better than nothing!

FITNESS MYTHS

Now that you are totally motivated and ready to improve your fitness, let's make sure you don't believe everything you have ever heard about working out. Here are some Fitness Myths adapted from CNNhealth.com that we need to get out of our heads:

MYTH: Women need to stay away from weights because it will make them bulk up.

TRUTH: It takes a ton of weight to make a woman bulk up. We just are not made to bulk up as much as men. Exercise experts believe that cardiovascular exercise and strength training are both valuable for maintaining a healthy weight. Women are not built to bulk up because of our hormones. We have a lovely hormone called estrogen that will keep us from getting bulky. Strength training helps decrease body fat, increase lean muscle mass, and burn calories more efficiently.

MYTH: Your weight is what you should hang your hat on.

TRUTH: You can be very healthy and weigh more than someone who is teeny tiny but has an unhealthy body. Don't let the scale decide how "healthy" you are.

MYTH: Longer exercise time burns more fat.

TRUTH: The most important focus during exercise is the total energy cost, or how many calories are burned during the activity. The faster you walk, step, or run the more calories you use per minute. If you are willing to work hard, you can exercise for shorter amounts of time and get better results than being on your elliptical for an hour at the same pace. High Intensity Interval Training is awesome and you can find programs online and at local gyms. The idea is to work out at higher intensity, take short breaks or change your speed, and actually spend less time at the gym.

MYTH: Protein shakes after a workout are vital.

TRUTH: Protein shakes, powders, and protein bars are good for those times where you just need something, but they are very low-quality food. You should not replace a full meal with a protein bar. You are much better off eating "real" food that is much less processed.

MYTH: You can work one area and spot reduce the fat there.

TRUTH: No matter how many crunches you do, you won't see a six-pack unless you put some cardio into your ab routine. There's a layer of fat resting on your abdominal muscles that you need to address also. Try to get an overall workout.

MYTH: As long as I get a half hour of exercise in, I can eat whatever I want for the rest of the day.

TRUTH: Working out will not make up for a bad diet. The important thing to remember is that making exercise a daily priority will go a long way in your overall health.[3]

MORE MYTHS AND TRUTHS FROM JESSIE:

MYTH: Exercise is one sure way to lose all the weight you desire.

TRUTH: Diet is half the battle—if not more important than exercise.

MYTH: If you're not going to work out hard and often, exercise is a waste of time.

TRUTH: Anything is better than nothing. Ten jumping jacks or walking to your mailbox is better than nothing. Just get up and move! You can even move while you watch your fave TV show or dance while you have those buds in your ears. ☺

MYTH: The health and fitness benefits of mind-body exercise like Tai Chi and yoga are questionable.

TRUTH: In fact, research showing the benefits of these exercises continues to grow. Tai chi, for example, has been shown to help treat lower-back pain and fibromyalgia. Improved flexibility, balance, coordination, posture, strength, and stress management are just some of the potential results of mind-body exercise.

MYTH: Home workouts are fine, but going to a gym is the best way to get fit.

TRUTH: Research has shown that some people find it easier to stick to a home-based fitness program. In spite of all the hype on trendy exercise programs and facilities, the "best" program for you is the one you will participate in consistently.

According to Carl Daikeler, CEO of Beachbody.com, "People who get in shape and stay in shape have three things in common: they work out at home, they weigh themselves once a week, and they eat a healthy breakfast."[4]

Most importantly, just remember that doing something is better than nothing. Exercise does not have to cost anything, take all your time, or be a boring chore. If you set yourself up for success by trying something you already like, start small with only ten to fifteen minutes a day, and choose to have the right mentality.

 YOU CAN DO IT *ANCHOR CLANKER!*

NUTRITION—YOU ARE WHAT YOU EAT!

Just the idea that we are what we eat makes perfect sense to me. I don't know about you, but when I eat too much candy or too many french fries, my body lets me know that I haven't made a good choice. I'm not saying that I'm anti-candy or fast food, but I want to plant an idea in your mind. Your body is built to handle that kind of stuff, but only in moderation.

My personal take on it is that as long as there is balance in your diet and you're eating healthy things most of the time, then you can certainly have a treat on Friday night at the movie with your friends.

Find the balance for you. What are your favorite veggies and fruit to eat? What are your favorite forms of protein? Are you a meat girl, or do you like boiled eggs? Find what's right for you. Develop your own opinions about how you eat and what you eat. How do you feel about your health right now? Do you want to change a few habits? It will take effort, but it will be worth it.

The first step toward healthy living is to get educated. Here are some awesome facts about food:

FOOD FACTS 101

- "Your brain depends on your stomach to signal that it's full, but that message takes 20 minutes to be delivered. So, slow down during meals, and you'll be less likely to eat too much."[5]

- "A 12-ounce can of regular Coke contains 39 grams of total sugar, which is about 9 1/3 teaspoons of sugar."[6]

- "Healthy eating in childhood and adolescence is important for proper growth and development and can prevent health problems such as obesity, dental cavities, iron deficiency, and osteoporosis."[7]

- "For teens, the recommended caloric intake is 2,100 calories, but it is important to base your diet on your level of physical activity. Depending on how active you are, you can determine how many daily calories are healthy for your weight and lifestyle."[8]

- "Business people, not nutritionists, plan fast-food meals. If you heavily entrust your nutritional needs to fast-food chains, your diet will have too much meat, fat, and salt. You'll still need to add dairy products, whole grains, fruits, and vegetables to your diet."[9]

- "It takes about twelve weeks after beginning to exercise and changing your diet to see measurable changes in your body."[10]

- "Research shows eating something before you bolt out the door in the morning—be it porridge, poached eggs, or peanut butter on toast—can help to boost your concentration, energy levels, and set you up for better eating throughout the day."[11] Even if you're not hungry, eat a small, nutritious breakfast.

- "Ten healthy, filling snacks: bananas, hard boiled eggs, nuts (almonds and pistachios), peanut butter, oatmeal, cottage cheese, plain Greek yogurt, sunflower seeds, apples, and watermelon, and natural fruit smoothies."[12]

INGREDIENTS YOU SHOULD ALWAYS AVOID

Do you know what is REALLY in the food you eat? If not, it is time to start being aware of exactly what is in your food. Let's talk about ingredients and food labels.

When you try to read food labels, you will notice a lot of funny words that do not sound like anything your grandmother would cook with. Many agree some of these ingredients can be harmful to your health. HealthierTalk.com gives us these ingredients to stay away from:

- BHA or BHT
- Parabens
- Partially Hydrogenated Oil
- Sodium Nitrate
- Caramel Coloring

- Castoreum

- Food dyes

- Hydrolyzed Vegetable Proteins

- High Fructose Corn Syrup

- Monosodium Glutamate (MSG)

- Aspartame

- Potassium Bromate

- Recombinant Bovine Growth Hormone (rBGH)

- Refined Vegetable Oil[13, 14]

Get in the habit of looking at food labels and avoiding these ingredients.

There are a few simple things I do that have really helped me with what I put in my body. Some fitness and nutrition people might have other ideas, but this is what I have found helps me. You get to decide what works for you, too. Just sayin'.

WHAT I LIKE TO PUT IN MY BODY

- I bought two 16-ounce water bottles with built in straws, and I drink a full 16 ounces of clean water first thing in the morning. This rehydrates your body after a beautiful night's rest and gets your brain ready for a new day.

- Since I'm a carbohydrate addict (breads, pasta, crackers, and cereals), I don't deny myself those glorious yummies—I just set limits. I can have toast, but only one slice. I can eat mac and cheese, but I have to have a full serving of broccoli first. I can have a bowl of cereal—but only one, and it has to be a "healthy" cereal like granola or Special K.

- This one is way hard, but I try not to eat after 7 p.m. What is it about cereal right before bed? I love that! But I notice I feel better when I don't eat late at night.

- I try to chew every bite twenty times. This helps me eat slower and digest all that delicious food better.

- I have healthy snacks with me in my purse, in my car, and in strategically placed spots in my house. If I snack a little, then I don't go overboard during meals. Almonds, dehydrated apples and strawberries, baby carrots, cutie oranges, jerky, and walnuts are my favorite snacks.

- Cheat day! I allow myself one day a week where I can eat whatever I want . . . within reason. This helps me not feel like I'm in a desert dying a slow, torturous death. I love to eat. What can I say? Being able to just relax for one day keeps me motivated all the other days.

- Making sure I get all the vitamins I need in a day through a smoothie in the morning is awesome, and I'm always surprised by how full I feel. Here are a few of glorious smoothie recipes:

ANTIOXIDANT SMOOTHIE: A JESSIE ORIGINAL

- 2 cups mixed frozen berries (9 ounces)
- 1 cup unsweetened pomegranate juice
- 1 cup water
- 1 cup ice

Blend together, and enjoy.

30 SECOND SMOOTHIE: ALSO A JESSIE ORIGINAL

- 1 orange
- Handful of washed strawberries
- Handul of spinach
- 1 cup ice

Cut the orange in half, peel it, throw it in the blender.
Add strawberries, spinach leaves, and ice. Blend. Yummy!

BANANA-OAT PROTEIN SMOOTHIE[15]

- 2 scoops of organic protein powder (available at any grocery store—just make sure it's labeled 100% organic)
- 2 tablespoons rolled oats
- 2 bananas
- 1 cup almond milk or regular milk
- 1/2 cup cold water

- 1 teaspoon honey

- 1/4 teaspoon cinnamon

- 5 ice cubes

Blend. Delicious. 😊

Small steps in the right nutritional direction can make a huge difference in how you feel—emotionally, mentally, and physically. It's all connected.

We are the stewards of our bodies. This means that we have a responsibility to take care of them. And I firmly believe that if we have discipline and do our best to take care of our bodies, they will take care of us. I'll say it again, if you don't have your health, you don't have anything. Be grateful for the incredible, miraculous, strong, awesome body you have!

✏ JOURNAL TIME

Let's get writing. Where did you put that smiley-face pencil?

What are some healthy foods you enjoy eating?

_____

_____

_____

What are some things you can start doing today that will benefit your health?

_____

_____

_____

_____

What are some things you know you need to change about your health habits?

_____

_____

_____

_____

CHALLENGE

Try making just two small changes in your diet and do some sort of physical activity every day this week—even if it's just walking around the block, cutting out fast food, and eating more vegetables. Choose to take hold of your health . . . it all comes down to our choices.

WRITE ABOUT YOUR EXPERIENCE:

_____

_____

_____

_____

CONFIDENT LADIES VALUE
THEMSELVES ENOUGH TO TAKE
CARE OF THEIR BODIES.

MOTHERHOOD

"The hand that rocks the cradle rules the world."

—WILLIAM ROSS WALLACE

I got married when I was twenty. I know—CRAZY! I never ever, EVER thought I would get married that young. Even though I was always excited about marriage and motherhood, I thought, *Yeah, maybe in my late, late twenties.* Then this darling man, named honey-bunny-bear-face (he loves it when I call him that . . . alright, his name is Jim) asked me to marry him, and I wanted to be with him forever! And voila—a new life plan was created. We had our first daughter when I was only twenty-one, and soon after, we decided to have another baby. I guess the memory of morning sickness, giant belly, swollen feet, and peeing my pants every time I sneezed just slipped my mind because I was so excited.

Pregnancy is a long road, girls; it takes a lot of energy to build kidneys and brains and ears and toes . . . from *scratch* . . . so keep that in mind when you're dating and thinking about marriage and motherhood. 😊

You may be thinking, *What does motherhood have to do with anything? Seriously, Jessie, I'm a teenager! That is way, way, waaay down the road for me.* If that's how you feel—GOOD. This topic will still be educational for you, though, so don't skip over it.

I have three goals for this chapter:

1   To help you more fully appreciate your mother or women in your life who have been like a mother a to you.

2   To help you think about whether motherhood is something you want in your future and imagine what you want that beautiful goal to look like.

3   To make it undeniably clear that it is so vital to your happiness and success in life to wait until the right time to become a mother.

Before we get into the nitty-gritty, I want to illustrate how awesome, and yet, challenging motherhood has been from my experience. You need to know that becoming a mother has been the best decision I have ever made—my two kids are my whole universe. I'm sure you have guessed that I am going to highly recommend this choice to you, and I am, but not until I give you plenty of information to think about.

Here are a few stories to give you a glimpse into the magical yet unpredictable world of mothering.

TALES *of* ADVENTURE!

CHILDREN CAN SEE GREAT BEAUTY—THEY CAN ALSO SHOCK YOU.

When my daughter Janessa was five, we were outside at a barbeque, and she came running up to me, BEYOND excited, and shrieks, "Mom, you have to come and see! It's the cutest potato bug I've ever seen!" (She tends to be a little bit dramatic—I have no idea where she gets it.) We headed over to look at the potato bug, and it was, in fact, a very cute potato bug—as potato bugs go. Then, from across the lawn, my almost-two-year-old son, Jackson, came thundering over to us. (We affectionately call him "The Tank" as he is about 35 pounds of pure love.) The Tank squatted down, surveyed this creature for about a half a second, wound up a fist and . . . SMACK DOWN! Poor bug— never had a chance.

The look of horror on my daughter's face was priceless. She just sat there, stunned and speechless. She would never do something so ruthless. I just took a step back and silently observed my offspring. I thought, *Wow, they came from the same parents—same gene pool and everything—and yet they couldn't be more different.*

Jackson . . . oh, sweet, insane Jackson.

Janessa . . . angelic, loving Janessa.

YOU SHOULD KNOW THAT YOUR CHILDREN WILL EMBARRASS YOU.

Just after my family moved to a brand-new neighborhood, we attended our first social event and were walking home. My husband and my two children were walking way ahead of me, and I had my back to them because I was trying to make friends with a lovely gal I'd just met.

I turned around to see my husband and my daughter, but no Jackson. I looked around for my son and saw him running toward a random house. Since I know my son oh so well, I knew exactly what was about to happen, so I took off in my high heels toward my son. (At least I was aerating this man's lawn for him. I am so nice.)

My son got to the door, rang the doorbell, and this adorable Asian man answered. I approached the front step just as my son yelled, "Hi!" and ran inside the house.

I was out of breath but already laughing when I get to the man. "I'm so sorry!" I pant. "Let me just grab him!"

Jackson saw me chasing him, so he thought it was a game. I was laughing because I couldn't help myself, so of course that just made him run faster.

He ran all the way through their entry-way, through their family room, and around the kitchen where this darling Asian family was sitting down having dinner. They had looks of horror on their faces, chopsticks frozen in mid-air as they watched this parade go by—me in my heels trying to claw for my son who is perpetually just out of my reach.

I finally cornered him in the pantry. Trying my best to stifle my giggles, I apologized not-so-convincingly to the family. I held my belly-laughing son by one arm and said, "I'm so sorry, I'm so sorry," only to discover that they did not speak English.

We got back to the front door where the adorable Asian man hadn't moved a muscle. I apologized profusely to him, and then, under my breath, I muttered, "And by the way . . . we're your new neighbors."

CHILDREN CAN BE SO VERY EDUCATIONAL.

In our home, we are firm believers in open and honest communication. I like to be very direct and bold with my children. I use correct terminology for things that do have a tendency to be uncomfortable but are important to discuss.

One night, we were having a family chat, and I decided it was time for my children to learn about the dangers of pornography. We were having a discussion about how if we see naked people on a screen of any sort, we immediately turn it off. We even used a karate analogy since karate is so important in our home. We were talking about how we block punches and defend ourselves. That is what we need to do with this poison called pornography—we have to actively block and fight the dangers of this horrific plague.

The next day, I was taking my son to preschool, and out of the blue, he said, "Hey mom, what's the name of the naked people again?"

I was perplexed for a minute, but then asked, "Pornography?"

"Yeah," he said. He continued to reiterate the lesson we'd had the night before. "We don't watch pornography. We block it cuz it's bad." He sat back in his chair after his inspiring lecture, content with his new-found knowledge.

I was so proud to know that he actually listens to the things I say. I gave him a hug and dropped him off at school. Five minutes later, I got a text from his teacher saying that Jackson was giving the entire class a wonderful lesson on blocking pornography. Yes, he does listen to me. Well done, my son.

Hopefully my darling children have enlightened your mind on the good times that can be had by all when you're a parent.

NOW LET'S LOOK AT THE SERIOUS SIDE OF MOTHERHOOD.

Being a parent is not all about fun and games. Here is a story about the harder side of motherhood.

When Janessa was almost two years old, I was thirty-six weeks into my next pregnancy—only four weeks to go. I was feeling really good. The first three months were horrible— throwing up five or six times a day and feeling so tired you could fall asleep in an aisle at Wal-Mart. Thankfully, that didn't last.

We decided to name the baby inside me Jordyn Haley. She was very active, and I already knew and loved her personality. She was feisty and sassy—a little spitfire. We would play this game where my husband would tap on my huge belly, and she would tap back. Seriously, I could feel her tapping inside of me. So freaking cool! She would only play that game with her dad, though. Whenever I tried it, she wouldn't respond. She just knew. I loved the idea of her being a daddy's girl. Oh, how I adored this baby that I hadn't even met yet.

One evening, really close to delivery, I realized that I hadn't felt Jordyn move all day long. And because she was so close to being born, I should have been feeling her move every hour or so. When I realized this, I rushed to the hospital. But it was too late. There was no heartbeat. My daughter had died inside of me. I delivered her the next day at the hospital, and we had a funeral for her. I had to place this beautiful little girl, MY beautiful little Jordyn, into a tiny coffin and bury her in the cold, January ground. It was one of the most excruciating experiences of my life.

I tell you this story to get you thinking about what motherhood means. It means sacrifice, physical discomfort, the possibility of accidents and tragedy, unattractive body changes, exhaustion, pain, and worry.

It also means feeling overwhelming happiness, giving your whole heart to another human, finding fulfillment and purpose in your life, being able to influence and create leaders who can do amazing things in this world, leaving a legacy, and experiencing a divine miracle that science will never be able to fully re-create.

Motherhood is one of the most beautiful opportunities for women on this earth. Because it is such a beautiful opportunity, motherhood comes with great responsibility.

TIMING IS EVERYTHING!

Having said all that mushy stuff about how wonderful motherhood is, I have seen the other side. I have worked with teen mothers who are single, depressed, and beyond stressed out about how they are going to take care of a child they have while still trying to get a high school diploma. So, it has to be said: If you think sex is worth the risk of getting pregnant as a teen, use that brilliant brain of yours, and think again. It's not! I know this is bold, but here are some statistics that back up my opinion.

According to DoSomething.org[1]:

- Three in ten teen American girls will get pregnant at least once before age twenty. That's nearly 750,000 teen pregnancies every year.

- Parenthood is the leading reason that teen girls drop out of school. More than half of teen mothers never graduate from high school.

- Less than 2 percent of teen moms earn a college degree by age thirty.

- The United States has one of the highest teen pregnancy rates in the western industrialized world.

- Eight out of ten teen dads don't marry the mother of their child.

- A sexually active teen who doesn't use contraceptives has a 90 percent chance of becoming pregnant within a year.

- Almost 50 percent of teens have never considered how a pregnancy would affect their lives.

- Each year, one in four teens contracts an STD (sexually transmitted disease).

A few more shocking stats:

- The sons of teenage mothers are 13 percent more likely to end up in prison.

- The daughters of teen mothers are 22 percent more likely to become teen mothers themselves.

- Children born to teenage mothers are 50 percent more likely to repeat a grade in school, have lower standardized test scores, and are more likely to drop out of high school than those born to older women.[2]

Don't become a statistic! Be smart and safe. You will be so much happier with yourself if you wait to have sex until you're married. WaitingTillMarriage.org says that couples have a 22 percent higher chance of staying married for the long term if they wait to have sex until after marriage.[3]

Just promise me one thing—here's where I get really bold. If you do find yourself pregnant, do NOT abort the baby. For the love, give him or her the opportunity to live. There are thousands of families who cannot have babies who would walk through fire to give your child a loving home and a good life. Abortion is murder, no matter how you slice it. That's a hill I will die on. I will happily go toe-to-toe with anyone who says otherwise. Having experienced two miscarriages and a stillbirth, I can't be silent about this. I value life too much. If you become pregnant, talk to a trusted adult—your parents, church leaders, your close friend's parents, teachers, your doctor—anyone you know you can trust, who cares about you, and can love you through this difficult process.

Choosing to abort a baby not only ends a life, but also has serious effects on the mother. These effects can be physical or mental.

AfterAbortion.org associates these after-effects with some women who have chosen or are forced into having an abortion: depression, post traumatic stress disorders, eating disorders, sexual dysfunction, alcohol/drug abuse, and abusive future relationships.[4]

If you find yourself pregnant from rape or incest, talk to a trusted adult. It's hard to think about, but these things do happen. The good news is that there are people who can help you through it.

Another thing to think about before becoming a mother is your ability to provide a loving home. If you feel that motherhood is not for you, that's okay. There are too many mothers in the world who are not good ones. That is a devastating truth that we have to face. Child abuse and abortion are two things I just don't handle well. It hurts my heart to the very core. Consider your ability to mother a child with love and patience before becoming a mother.

We just talked about some very serious issues here, but I hope those thoughts will help you have respect for and cherish the opportunity to create, nurture, and cherish another person's life.

 DUDLEY DO-RIGHT, MAMA BEAR, OVER AND OUT.

Enough of that. You are a teenager and life is good. All I can tell you is that, from my experience, being a good mother is the only thing that will really matter to me when I'm ninety, sitting in the nursing home, eating my Jell-O. It has been the hardest, most amazing, most rewarding choice I have ever made. I am so proud and thankful that my kids are growing up in a loving home with a mom and dad who love them more than anything else in the world. That picture is worth the wait, ladies.

LET'S TALK ABOUT MOTHERHOOD AWESOMENESS!

Here are some awesome visuals that can help you develop a healthy, positive image of what motherhood could look like in your dazzling future.

TOOL #14

Record Your Mom Dreams

Yes, ladies, go get your favorite writing utensil, please. 😊

What are some things you admire about your mom and/or other mother figures in your life?

_____

_____

_____

_____

_____

What are some things that you do for your mother that make her day?

_____

_____

_____

_____

_____

What are some things you COULD do for her to show her you appreciate her—things you might not have done before?

_____

_____

_____

_____

What are some things your mom does for you that make your day?

_____

_____

_____

_____

What are some of your favorite memories of your childhood that you might want to re-create in your own home someday?

_____

_____

_____

_____

Write down five things you want to do with your kids when you're a mother. Going to the zoo, to the park, Disneyland, playing hide and seek, etc.

_____

_____

_____

_____

_____

What do you hope your kids say about you at your funeral? Morbid, I know but it's good to think ahead. ☺ What kind of memories do you hope they may have?

_____

_____

_____

_____

_____

_____

_____

_____

What kind of legacy do you want to leave for your posterity—that is your kids and grandkids and so on? Again, we are really thinking ahead here!

_____

_____

_____

_____

_____

_____

_____

_____

_____

_____

_____

CONFIDENT, CLASSY LADIES HAVE RESPECT FOR LIFE.

 CHALLENGE

This week, take a look at the moms you admire in your life. Take notice of what their daily lives are like, and think about what it takes to be a good mom. You could even interview a few moms you look up to. It may be fun and surprising to see what they have to say. Getting a healthy image in your mind of what you want motherhood to look like is a great way to plan for that beautiful dream to come true—when the time is right. Think about your future . . . it all comes down to our choices.

WRITE ABOUT YOUR EXPERIENCE:

_____

_____

_____

_____

_____

_____

_____

_____

POSITIVE MENTAL ATTITUDE

"If you realized how powerful your thoughts are you would never think a negative thought again."

—UNKNOWN

I f you are near your computer or smartphone, watch the video for this chapter before you read another line. If you can't, here is a quick illustration.

You get up in the morning, look in the mirror at your crazy bedhead and sleepy eyes, and think, *Oh-my-lanta, Penelope, don't you dare go outside today. You will give your old neighbor a heart attack! You look absolutely hideous. Your kneecaps are protruding. What is going on with your hair? It looks like the scarecrow from* The Wizard of Oz *lost all of his straw stuffing and glued it onto your head. And don't even think about talking to Fredrico today, that hot Spanish guy in math; he is so not into you and why would he ever be? You are a disaster, and no one wants to date a disaster. Bottom-line, you might as well go take a trip to Zimbabwe and disappear.*

How are you feeling right now? Do you feel all warm and fuzzy? Are there fluffy bunnies and rainbows in your heart because of the positivity I just created? Or do you want to punch me in the face? Man, words like that are so depressing! Words like that are hurtful, sad, lame, annoying, and just negative.

Let's try this again. You get up and look at that same crazy hair and sleepy eyes and tell yourself, *Wow, Penelope! I cannot believe how shiny your hair is today! I just love your fingernail polish—it's so colorful and decorative. I don't know if I've ever told you this, but your clavicles are truly splendid. Have I ever said that I really love being your friend? I just love hanging out with you because I feel like I can totally be myself and be happy. You make me laugh. Your smile just brightens any room! Oh, and your spinach brownies are marvelous. You are a culinary genius.*

Now how do you feel? Is that better? I just want to take a big sigh of relief and relax. Words have power. Do you concur? I know that you had to feel something when hypothetical Penelope was chewing herself out. Words create emotions. Our words have the power to breathe fresh life into us, and our words have power to suck the life right out of us—remember that idea from my mentor, Josh Shipp, about there being two types of people in the world—breathers and suckers? Ask yourself again: *Do I want to be a breather or a sucker?*

Would you ever talk to one of your friends like that? Probably not. How often do we talk to ourselves that way, though?

The most important part of this idea is to visualize yourself standing in front of a mirror and talking to yourself the way I was talking to Penelope in the first example. How often do we tell ourselves that we are fat, ugly, stupid, weird, awkward, annoying, or just not good enough? Talking to ourselves with kindness is something we need to exercise—just like that muscle that gets stronger when we exercise it, we get stronger when we exercise our positive mental attitude.

If we constantly create a negative atmosphere in our minds by poisoning ourselves with harsh and destructive words, then all we are going to get is a harsh, destructive life. We are what we think.

Be kind to yourselves, ladies!

Choosing to be optimistic and positive is a life-skill you can learn. It's not necessarily a genetic quality you're born with.

Here's a cool excerpt from an article that introduces the idea of Optimistic Exploratory Styles. Naming these different styles can help us process and make sense of bad situations.

Imagine two students who receive the same poor grade on an exam. The first student thinks, "I'm such a failure! I always do poorly in this subject. I can't do anything right!" The second student thinks, "This test was difficult! Oh well, it's just one test in one class. I tend to do well in other subjects." These students are exhibiting two types of what psychologists call "explanatory styles." Explanatory styles reflect three attributions that a person forms about a recent event. Did it happen because of me (internal) or something or someone else (external)? Will this always happen to me (stable) or can I change what caused it (unstable)? Is this something that affects all aspects of my life (pervasive) or was it a solitary occurrence (limited)?[1]

Let's clarify what this idea means in daily life. When you face a challenge, and you will, you have the power to choose how you handle that situation. Here is an example of how you can change your thought process so that challenge doesn't shatter you.

I speak in high school assemblies all over the country. After a presentation in Azle, Texas, I was chatting with a group of girls. They were taking turns singing for me, and they all had beautiful voices! One girl was particularly shy, but her friends were egging her on to sing for me. Another girl turned to her and said, "Why would Jessie want to hear you?" This harsh comment made this darling girl start crying. I saw her and gave her a hug.

She told me what this other girl had said, and I asked her, "What's the truth? Are you a good singer?"

She thought for a second, but then confidently stated, "Yes, I am!"

In that split second, she made a choice. She chose to dismiss that negative poison from the other girl, and she zeroed in on the truth. It all comes down to choices. We can choose to beat ourselves up when we make mistakes or when someone is unkind, or we can choose to find the positive side.

One area of positive or negative energy that constantly nags at us girls is . . . self-image. Let's address this huge issue.

WHAT IS "BEAUTY" TO YOU?

As I was growing up, I competed in a lot of pageants. I won the title of Miss Pleasant Grove 2001, as well as Miss Congeniality. As a married lady, I competed in the Mrs. Utah pageant, not even making the top eight, but was voted by my friends in the competition to receive Mrs. Congeniality. I was the director for the Miss Kaysville pageant for two years, and I was a field director for the Miss Utah organization for one year. I have also M.C.'d and judged dozens of pageants.

I am grateful for my experiences with pageants. I learned interviewing skills, how to perfectly set a curl with the right hairspray to heat ratio, and how to "glide" on a stage (insert Sandra Bullock in *Miss Congeniality* visual). I also learned something that is infinitely more important and more meaningful to me: I learned that there are so many more important things in this world besides beauty! There are so many different ways to feel confident besides being outwardly beautiful.

As a girl and a teen, I was very aware that I was no glamouricious runway model like Gisele or Heidi Klum, but I am here to tell you that I AM BEAUTIFUL, and I'm not afraid to shout it from the mountaintops. Being aware of the fact that a fashion editor might not put my face on the cover of Vogue magazine has nothing to do with my beauty. This awareness has been such an incredible blessing to me. Let me explain why.

When we can separate what we think of as "beauty" from how we look on the outside, we actually give ourselves permission to FIND "beauty" and power and awesomeness in other areas of our lives.

I have many gifts that mean so much to me. Honestly, if I had to choose between being a good mother/singer/author/speaker and being a drop-dead gorgeous fashion model, I would choose the first option in a heartbeat! Accepting that outward beauty is not my most important attribute has given me the priceless gift of freedom—freedom to explore many other talents and opportunities that bring me so much happiness.

That is all I want for you. I want you to know that you can define what beauty means. You get to choose how you see yourself. You can choose to celebrate your healthy, strong, powerful body, or you can destroy it by trying to compete with airbrushed, photoshopped magazine models who do not now, nor will they ever, look like that in real life. Your definition of beauty is your choice. Repeat after me. I AM BEAUTIFUL. Say it out loud. Say it every day, and choose to believe it!

It's important to clarify here that I am such a girly girl. I love dressing up, playing with make-up, high heels, hair styling, and all that. I'm completely comfortable stating that it's so fun to be a girl and to celebrate that by primping, polishing, and pampering ourselves.

The point I'm making is that there is yet again a balance we must find with outward beauty and our priceless inner beauty. Learning to love ourselves for more than our photogenic quality is a skill that will serve you now and when you're ninety years old competing in the nursing home beauty pageant!

Learning to find and cherish other gifts at a young age is such a valuable and fun thing! I loved learning that I could make people laugh, I learned to really polish my talent of singing, I developed a great work ethic so that I could accomplish so many dreams, and I learned to really be a good friend and listen to other people. Those are gifts that I don't know I would have developed if I got all my attention and validation from my looks. So, what I'm saying is, sometimes when you discover a "weakness," that might just be the thing that helps you discover your strengths.

I have met with many women who were professional models in their younger years. These completely stunning women have told me that as they get older and their outward beauty starts to fade, their self-esteem suffers. They realize that they have based a lot of their worth on how they look.

This is where the danger of makeup, hair styles, plastic surgery, and outward beauty come into play. Those things by themselves are not evil or bad, but if you turn to those things to find your worth and happiness, you will be disappointed—I promise. Worth and happiness cannot ever come from those things—it has to come from within. All of our girly "toys" like eye-shadow and nail polish are just fun activities and tools we can use to accentuate our already existing awesomeness.

An easy test to find out if you place too much emphasis on how you look is to go out with no makeup on. Can you still love yourself and feel happy about your life in general? If that thought just made you cringe, let me just insert here that it's hard for me, too, but it's an easy way to do a self-check on where we are placing our worth. Think about it.

If this is something that resonates with you, I suggest that after you put on your makeup in the morning, don't check yourself out again the rest of the day. Instead, focus on moving forward on your dreams. Work hard at school because you know if you do, you'll get into that culinary college and become that gourmet chef you want to be! Focusing on real, meaningful, important things in your life can help you open yourself up to all sorts of wondrous things.

Who knows, maybe you'll meet a new friend who you'll have a blast hanging out with. Maybe you'll nail your interview for that job you really wanted. Maybe that boy will say "Hi" to you today. Maybe you will score three goals in the soccer game tonight. Maybe you will ace your history test. Maybe you'll make cheerleader. Maybe you'll invent a retractable central vacuum cord (pretty please). Maybe you'll start a non-profit organization that helps orphans in Tanzania. Maybe you'll even learn something new today—one idea that changes how you see the world. Now that is a positive thought!

PINK JELL-O BRAIN

Creating a positive mental attitude is about making a choice to think positively. Therefore, if there is something that fills you with a negative thought or makes you feel low and unworthy . . . get that thought out of your brain immediately, and replace it with a happy thought. (See tool below.)

Think of your brain like a huge barrel of pink Jell-O. (I have a secret dream of swimming in Jell-O . . . just like in the movie *Cloudy with a Chance of Meatballs*). You want to add things into that Jell-O that are positive and happy and fun and exciting and have a purpose. Keep that Jell-O free of toxic chemicals that will totally ruin your beautiful pink Jell-O. Are you liking this analogy? I love Jell-O.

You have control over your work ethic; you have control over how you see the world, just like my hero—Oprah Winfrey. One of my favorite quotes from this glorious woman is a simple one. She said, "I know for sure that what we dwell on is who we become." I don't know about you, but when I spend time dwelling on negative things, frustrating things, and/or stressful things—all I feel is negative, frustrated, and stressed! Oprah is right. We have control over our attitude, we have control over where we find our worth, we have control over forgiving others, we have control over the kind of words that come out of our mouths, we have control over our happiness, and we have control over our attitude! Yes, I know I said that twice. 😊 Sometimes having a good attitude is dang hard to do—I can attest to that—but we do have control over it.

Can you guess what I'm going to say next . . . yep, you are so smart—IT'S LIKE A MUSCLE! The more you exercise it, the stronger it gets. The more you practice positive thinking, the stronger and better you will be at using a positive attitude in your life. You are exercising your positive attitude muscle.

The perfect person to illustrate this idea is Bethany Hamilton. She is one incredible gal. For anyone who doesn't know of her, she is the surfer in the book and movie *Soul Surfer* who lost her left arm in a shark attack. One of my favorite quotes from this lovely leader is, "Courage doesn't mean you don't get afraid. Courage means you don't let fear stop you." She is so brave. She got back in the water to surf only a few weeks after her attack. A. Freaking. Mazing!

She also said, "Your looks do not define who you are." That horrifying experience would be really hard for a lot of us normal people. Bethany is not a normal person. She looked her fears square in the eye and pushed right past them. She made a conscious choice to stay positive and move forward. She is my hero.

 TOOL #15

Happy Arsenal

When you have a negative thought come into your head . . .

- I'm ugly.

- I'm so stupid.

- That guy will never be into me.

- I'll never be good enough to please my dad.

- My acne ain't goin' nowhere, might as well get a pen out and play connect the dots.

- Dyslexia will haunt me for.ev.er.

- I'm weird.

- I don't fit in.

- My teacher WANTS me to fail this class.

- No one wants to hang out with me.

- I didn't make the soccer team because I suck.

- I'm not tall enough to be a good dancer, so I won't even try.

- Take the drugs—life sucks anyway.

. . . kick that thought right into the next galaxy. Literally say, out loud, "You are not welcome in my brain!" Saying it out loud will create strength within you.

Once you dismiss that unwelcome thought, you instantly REPLACE that poison with something awesome, wonderful, exciting, and positive!

This requires you to create a "HAPPY ARSENAL." Always keep four or five exciting, positive thoughts in your arsenal at all times. Write them down in your planner or your notes on your phone. Five awesome memories, goals, thoughts, or anything that makes you feel HAPPY:

They can be simple phrases that help you feel powerful, such as:

- I am strong.

- I am capable.

- I am powerful.

- I am beautiful.

- I am fun.

- I am kind.

- I have a good heart.

- I care about other people.

- I deserve happiness because I am a good person.

Or maybe you put memories in your happy arsenal. Find strong memories that evoke powerful feelings in you. Think of Harry Potter trying to do this when Professor Lupin is trying to teach him how to do a patronus charm . . . *Expecto Patronum!* That's actually a great analogy for a chapter about positive thinking . . . don't allow those dementors into your heads, girls. Keep them out with the patronus charm that requires a really happy thought. A big thank you to J. K. Rowling for a perfect metaphor!

- Your family's trip to Disneyland when you were thirteen

- That time you made the winning basket at the school game

- When that adorable little boy you used to babysit told you that you were his hero

- Your goal of designing clothes when you grow up

- Christmas morning

- Your upcoming shopping trip with your older sister

- That time your teacher told you that you were so smart and had a bright future in science

Your happy arsenal can be filled with anything that evokes a deep, real sense of happiness, peace, or excitement. Make a list, and keep it where you will see it often.

🖉 JOURNAL TIME

This is so important—let's jot down some happiness right now. Write down ten awesome thoughts. Hot-pink pen please.

_____

_____

_____

_____

_____

_____

_____

👢 TALES *of* ADVENTURE!

Let's keep going with the pageant examples. I saved this little sweetheart for the grand finale of this chapter because it's just that good. (By good, I mean entertainingly ridiculous.)

As you know, all my life I competed in pageants. I started competing when I was six years old (not *Toddlers and Tiaras*—no fake teeth, spray-tans, or ratted hair extensions—I solemnly swear). I enjoyed them as a kid because I made a whole bunch of new friends who I saw every year. I loved working hard, dressing up, and singing. Some might say I have a slightly competitive spirit. Which is true . . . if by "slightly," you mean "significantly." It was also one of the few times my mom and I could hang out and get along really well, because we were both doing something we liked and having a blast!

I was fortunate, too, in that my mom wasn't a crazy stage mother. She would always tell me, "Jessie, we are not here to win. That would be nice, but we are here to have fun and learn good things."

I believed her, so I just did my best and had a fiesta doing it. When I was ten years old, I told my mom, "Pageants are fun, but I'm ready to move on. Let's try other things."

"Okay, Jessie," she said. "Let's go out with a bang! We'll sign up for the International Cinderella Scholarship Pageant in Oklahoma City!"

It was an open pageant, so anyone could enter. There were about two million girls at this week-long competition. (That might be a slight exaggeration; maybe it was more like two thousand . . . okay, even that might be pushing things, but let's go with it—makes the story more dynamic.) When I was ten, I had a killer work ethic and crazy ambition, which meant I was determined to win this thing. I thought, *If this is my last pageant, that crown is MINE—no question about it!* I had my talent perfected, interview questions polished, and my modeling categories were . . . let's be honest . . . flawless. I was *going* to win!

My mom and I left our hotel in downtown Oklahoma City and were headed to the first event—the interview. We were walking really fast—couldn't be late on the first day of competition! My mom was fluffing my hair, and I was going through interview questions in my mind—getting my head in the game. Just then, I noticed something out of the corner of my eye. *Cinderella!* Or rather, the winner of the pageant from the previous year. This was the girl that all the two million . . . I mean two thousand . . . girls at the pageant wanted to BE at the end of the week.

So, I'm staring at her as she gets out of her limo, everything moving in slow motion, her glowing blonde hair flowing in the wind, hundreds of girls rushing around her, pushing and shoving and stampeding to get her autograph. (I might have imagined the shoving.) I softly smiled and thought to myself, *Wow—that's going to be me! I am so excited!* I was still walking fast, mesmerized and lost in thought, until I finally turned my head to focus on where I was going, and BAM! It sounded a little bit like a skull cracking against a flagpole. Maybe even

KICKING THE TRASH out of some poor girl's nose bones in two places. And wouldn't you know it? That nose belonged to me.

Me! Jessie's nose! Jessie's face! And yes, let's take just a moment to visualize this together, shall we? Allow me the opportunity to re-live it. I collided head-on with a six-inch-wide flagpole! My glory days as a graceful, poised debutant. CRASH AND BURN!

Needless to say, I did not win the pageant. Something about two black eyes and a schnoz packed with bloody wads of gauze. Whatever. (Pardon me for a moment. Wince. Biting of the fist.)

I can laugh about it now. However, in that moment, and for the rest of that week, especially when girls would come up to me and exclaim, "Are you the girl who ran into the flagpole? Oh, you poor thing. Well, better luck next year!" I found no humor in the situation. I was devastated.

When we got home, I announced, "Mom, I don't want to do this anymore."

She chuckled under her breath and answered, "I know, Jessie, that was the plan. We were only going to do one more pageant, remember? You wanted to go out with a bang, and you sure did!"

Burning her with my smoldering glare, I said, "No, I mean all of it. I don't want to sing anymore or dance anymore or try anything! If I'm going to work that hard and something like THAT happens, I am not interested!" Then I threw myself dramatically onto my bed and wept.

My mother, in her infinite wisdom, said, "Jessie, I'm glad this happened."

I sat up stiffly, ready to scream, when she continued. "Setbacks are a part of life. Bad things are going to happen, and you have to decide right now how you are going to handle them. Are you going to let life defeat you, or are you going to suck it up and learn from it?"

She was absolutely right. (Although, at the time, I sure wasn't going to admit it!) I am so thankful I learned this lesson at a young age, because now, when I experience trials, I am stronger for it.

I'm sure you have had times where you felt beaten down, frustrated, or embarrassed. Every human on the planet can relate to that! How do you react? Is it easy for you to pick yourself up and let it go? Or does it shatter you? I have felt shattered. It's no fiesta, but if you can make a decision right now to stay positive, you will be better prepared when the next struggle comes.

So, you get to choose. The next time you are teased or bullied, or the next time you try something new, only to find that it's not for you . . . will you let it define you and tether you to the ground, or will you use it to help you get tough and determined—to become who you were meant to be? Our struggles can be just the thing that propels us to where we are supposed to be. They can help us find our destiny. Are you going to use your setbacks to grow stronger? Or will you let them drag you down and destroy you? It is not easy, but the choice must be made now.

The point of this chapter is to help you think about embarrassing moments, setbacks, or struggles in a different way. Just like my pageant experience—it was NOT funny in the moment, but now (19.5 years later, more or less) I can laugh at it and see that there was a good lesson to be learned. We have to learn to laugh. Laughing not only makes us happy, but it burns calories. Bonus! Plus, everyone likes to be around someone with a good attitude. Simple question—would you rather hang around someone who's negative and whiny with a victim mentality or with somebody who is happy and excited about living? My point exactly. We can choose to have a positive mental attitude!

Now here's a good exercise for when you have those embarrassing moments and setbacks. Notice how I never use the word failure—I don't believe in failure. You only fail if you fail to learn something from the experience.

TOOL #16

How Serious Is It?

On a scale from one to ten . . . how serious is your current challenge?

1 2 3 4 5 6 7 8 9 10

One being, your ice cream cone melted and now your hands are sticky. Ten being, your house is a fiery inferno, you can hear the dog howling inside, your mother is in the hospital dying from brain cancer, your ex-best friend just hacked into your bank account and stole your life savings, you've become permanently blinded after being trapped underneath a pile of burning rubble, and your dad filed for divorce as he boarded a plane to Zimbabwe with his new girlfriend, Helga. All within the last ten minutes. THAT kind of ten.

So, how serious is it? Are the things that truly matter intact? Being grateful for the things we DO have helps us to keep our lives in perspective and to stay positive.

If your whole world is shattered over tripping down the hall and getting laughed at, then I want you to think about all the kids around the world who would literally give their right arm just to have the chance to walk . . . or even trip . . . in your comfy, clean shoes.

TALES of ADVENTURE!

When I was thirteen, my parents sat my brothers and me down and told us they were getting a divorce. In all honesty, my brothers and I reacted with the word, "Finally." Because of the tension between my parents, our family was really unhappy.

During the transition, my relationship with my mom was strained. Even though we had a lot in common, we were also night and day different. When she moved out, my two brothers and I lived with our dad, and things were much better. We were a happier family—all of us. My mom was still involved in my life, and our relationship was a bit better than it had been.

One day, I was hanging out with a family member I really liked and respected. Out of the blue, he said, "Jessie, I am so impressed with you. You have overcome so much. I can't imagine how hard it must have been for you to have your mother abandon you."

The word *abandon* hit me like a ton of bricks. I knew it was completely untrue, but my own little shoulder devil started whispering ugliness in my ear: "He's right. She did abandon you. She was selfish and didn't want to be your mother anymore."

I'm saying it again, just to make sure you understand how important this is—I knew it wasn't true! But, I CHOSE to believe that it was. I CHOSE to start being angry at my mother. I CHOSE to push her out of my life. I CHOSE to be mean and closed off, to have a surface relationship, to not let her into my world, and to be a complete brat. What I didn't realize about all these choices was that they would come with a price. Suddenly, I was obsessed and consumed with anger. I wanted to talk about it all the time, so whenever my friends and I were together, I'd figure out a way to bring it up in conversation. "Oh my gosh, you guys you would not believe what my crazy mom did this week." And then I wondered why my friends didn't want to hang out with me as much. It's annoying and draining to hang out with angry people.

I even exaggerated things to be much worse than they really were. For example, when I went to prom and my date came to pick me up, my parents weren't at the house. My date asked where they were. I shrugged, "I don't know." Which was technically true, but I left out the fact that I had forgotten to even tell them it was prom.

A couple of weeks later, my mom asked, "So, when is prom?" I told her I'd already gone.

"Why didn't you tell me? I wanted to be there to take pictures! I didn't know when it was!" she said.

You would think I'd acknowledge that she felt bad about it. You would also think I'd acknowledge that it was ME who didn't let her know I was going to Prom, but I didn't. I hissed to my friends, "I can't believe my mother! She doesn't care about me at all! She wasn't even there to take pictures of me leaving for the dance!" I have a hard time believing how cruel, heartless, and selfish I was. I never thought about how much I was hurting my mother.

Through all of this, she tried her very best to be patient and loving with me. "What's wrong, Jessie? Why won't you let me in?" she would ask. She tried to come to my school events or other activities I was participating in, but I'd ignore her effort. I also ignored that I had chosen to buy into a lie. What I was angry about wasn't even based on reality, and I knew it.

After this had gone on for years, I had a life-changing moment. It wasn't some earth-shattering event. No prophetic vision or ghosts from the grave. I was simply sitting on my bed, being angry at my mom for a recent episode, when suddenly, these thoughts crossed my mind:

Where is your anger getting YOU, Jessie? What is it doing for YOU? How is it helping YOU?

I thought about those questions for a long time and slowly realized that the only result of my anger was that I was angry. I had spent so much time and energy being mad, when I could have been having fun and living life. My choice to be angry was holding me back from being HAPPY. I couldn't believe it! It was as if a blindfold was ripped off my eyes, and suddenly, I could see clearly. I was the one who had tied that blindfold and intentionally stayed in the dark. This epiphany was amazing to me. I cried my eyes out because I was overwhelmed by the feeling that I had the power to remove that blindfold. That day, sitting on my bed, I made a decision that changed my life forever. I chose to let it go. I chose to drop-kick that crappy brick backpack out of my life, and it worked.

I called my mom and said, "I don't want to dig through all the mud and sort everything out. I just want to let it go and start fresh. I'm so sorry for how I've treated you, and I forgive you. Can we move forward and be friends?"

We weren't best friends the next day or even the next month. It took a while, but once I decided to let go of those self-defeating behaviors, it was so much easier. It was like sucking in a lung full of fresh air after feeling buried beneath a heap of manure. Stinky, smothering, damp manure. (Like that visual? Eeewww.)

Something else happened that was pretty cool. I learned that I needed to forgive myself, too, and move on. So I did. Every day, I could feel myself letting go and becoming stronger. I would visualize dropping that brick backpack off that cliff, and it helped heal my soul and my relationship with my mom.

I am happy to report that my mom and I are now BFFs! Does that mean we always agree . . . that we are one hundred percent compatible? No. It means that I don't judge her anymore. I accept her for who she is, and I show appreciation for the good things she does. I love her. I CHOOSE to love her.

I don't know if you can relate to this story. But one thing we do all have in common is that, as humans, we tend to hold onto those stupid bricks: anger, resentment, fear, judgment, jealousy, worry, stress, and pain. We act like these things are lifelines; but really, they are balls and chains, or bricks adding to other bricks in a backpack. We MUST learn to let it go if we want to be happy. You are the only one holding yourself back by choosing to have these bad feelings. I know that sounds harsh, because whatever you are feeling is most likely based on something real—something that really hurts. However, it's still a choice. You either hold onto it and make excuses, or choose to get rid of it and move on.

My point, in case you missed it, is that you are responsible for your happiness. No one can give it to you; you have to fight for it.

✏ JOURNAL TIME

Pull that hot-pink pen out of your hair, and let's go!

What poisonous words do you say to yourself?

_____

_____

_____

What positive words could you say instead?

_____

_____

What negative beliefs do you hold onto that keep you from happiness?

_____

_____

_____

Why do you hold onto them?

_____

_____

What do you need to do to let it go?

_____

_____

_____

What makes you feel the greatest joy?

_____

_____

_____

🔩 TOOL #17

THREE QUESTIONS

1   Are you as sincere as you know how to be?

2   Are you as kind as you know how to be?

3   Are you the best sister/niece/friend/second cousin once removed/person that you know how to be?

If you can answer "yes" to these questions, feel confident. You cannot control other people. Some humans are going to say mean things and do mean things, and you have no control over them. What you DO have control over is how you react and whether or not you're going to be angry or move on. Anytime you get hurt by a rude comment at school, or someone spreads an ugly rumor or judges you harshly, tell yourself, "I am as nice as I know how to be, and that is good enough." That's a great mantra to repeat over and over in your head.

If your answer to any of those questions is "no," then remedy that. Don't give empty compliments. Quit gossiping. Tell your family you love them. Stop criticizing, and START being the kind of friend you would want to have. This can be difficult, but it must be done, and YOU are the only one who can make it happen. No excuses. Don't wait for someone else to push you in that direction. Take control of your emotions and your happiness! "FEEL THE RAIN ON YOUR SKIN . . . " Sorry. I get a little carried away.

It's all a process. That is what life is about! We are all here to experience joy AND pain and to learn something along the way. Let go of your self-defeating behaviors, and be willing to forgive. It's the best gift you can give yourself.

CHALLENGE

Try the Happy Arsenal Tool. See if you can go one day and then one week without allowing negative thoughts to stay in your mind for longer than five seconds. Kick them out fast! Choose to control your mind and its positive or negative attitude . . . it all comes down to our choices.

WRITE ABOUT YOUR EXPERIENCE:

_____

_____

_____

_____

_____

_____

_____

_____

Confident, powerful ladies choose to take responsibility for their happiness.

PERSONAL POWER

"IF YOU'RE STILL LOOKING FOR THAT ONE PERSON WHO CAN CHANGE YOUR LIFE, LOOK IN THE MIRROR."

—ROMAN PRICE

Think back to Skill #1: Confidence. Remember how confidence is your foundation as you build a great life? Well, personal power is the cement that holds that foundation together. So when you exercise your personal power, your confidence remains rock solid. This chapter is very important to me personally because this is the one skill I wish I had learned as a teen. I want so badly for you to learn it and recognize your own, divine personal power. It's already in us; we were born with it. Sometimes we just need to give ourselves permission to use it.

In this chapter, we are going to learn how to keep our personal power strong through five lessons:

- Processing our emotions in a healthy way

- Not giving our power away

- Removing the bully factor

- Managing our stress

- Steering clear of toxic relationships

We are going to start this chapter out a little differently than the others. Let's take a minute and see where you are with your personal power at this moment. Be honest with yourself; there are no wrong answers.

✏ JOURNAL TIME

(No skipping! Pull out your fuzzy, purple feather pen.)

Do you feel powerful?

_____

_____

Do you believe that you could be powerful?

_____

_____

Do you want to be powerful?

_____

_____

What is your definition of a "powerful" human?

_____

_____

Now let's add on to those questions by making some strong, declarative statements about our rights.

YOUR OWN "BILL OF RIGHTS"

Now, I want you to write down what you believe your rights are.

If you are thinking, *Explain your gibberish, Jessie*, okay, Tijuana Taxi, I hear ya. Here is what your Bill of Rights is about.

Do you have the right to free speech?

Do you have the right to be free from persecution?

Do you have the right to be safe from predators?

Do you have the right to say "NO"?

Do you have the right to fight if you feel endangered?

Do you have the right to practice the religion of your choosing?

Do you have the right to be happy?

Do you have the right to be treated with respect?

Do you have the right to be safe and healthy?

Now I want you to write it out. "I have the right to . . ." Writing out the full sentence is an empowerment exercise for you, and, yes, say it with me . . . the more you exercise this confidence muscle, the stronger it will get.

✏ JOURNAL TIME

MY BILL OF RIGHTS

I have the right to:

_____

_____

_____

_____

_____

_____

_____

_____

As we go through this chapter, you'll come up with more rights to add to this list. Turn back here, and please add your awesome ideas!

What happens when we or other people don't follow our Bill of Rights? Let me illustrate.

PROCESS YOUR EMOTIONS IN A HEALTHY WAY

Do you know someone who is angry or bitter? I'm sure you do—we all do. I guarantee that these people have been hurt. They have not upheld their Bill of Rights, or someone else has violated it. We all have an inborn Bill of Rights, whether we know it or not. We are born with that Jiminy Cricket in our heads telling us what is right and what is wrong. When bad things happen to us or we make bad choices, there's a reason why we feel hurt, and why we have those things called emotions.

Those difficult experiences and the emotions they create are hard to get rid of. Here we go with the brick backpack again. That time your friend told you that you were not smart enough to make the debate team—another brick goes into the backpack. That time when you shot for your dream of joining Disney on Ice but didn't make the cut—another brick goes into the pack. Tripping down the hall, getting dumped, lying to your parents and getting caught, spreading a viscous rumor, hearing rumors spread about you, the images you can't get out of your head because your friend showed you some pornography, your eating disorder, compromising your Bill of Rights when your boyfriend went too far, your dad yelling at you for being lazy, feeling depressed, the death of your beloved chinchilla named Pappy . . . brick by brick by brick, our pack becomes too heavy to lift.

That backpack is exhausting; it makes you cynical, negative, pessimistic, and untrusting. And worst of all—you don't know how to get rid of it.

I am here to tell you that it's as easy as taking that emotion-filled backpack off your worn-out shoulders and drop-kicking it out of your life. Ouch! Maybe throwing it over a cliff is a better visual.

TOOL #18

Emotion Processing—Get It Out

Imagine taking all of those feelings of rejection, embarrassment, anger, frustration, sadness, being overwhelmed, stress, violation, being out of control, etc., and picture yourself at the edge of a massive cliff looking out at the never-ending ocean. It's sunset; the water is all shiny, golden, and glorious. You are alone with your ginormous backpack full of bricks. Look at each brick, feel the feelings that each one has created in you—really allow yourself to feel it. Cry and scream if you want. Take that backpack, and drop it over the edge of the cliff. Watch it fall all the way to the water. It makes a huge splash and is lost to Davey Jones' locker (had to throw a *Pirates of the Caribbean* reference in there).

Then, say out loud to yourself or to the person who hurt you, "I forgive you. I am moving on." Say it and mean it the best you can. If those bricks ever try to come back into your thoughts, don't allow them to stay in your head. Dismiss them, and then say it again, "I forgive you. I am moving on."

The most important thing to remember about pain is that time can heal a lot of wounds. Give yourself some time, give yourself some space, and really try to figure out what will help you heal the fastest and the most effectively. Is it going up the canyon, being still and listening to the leaves and the wind? Is it listening to your favorite music? Is it watching your favorite movie? Is it reading your favorite book? Meditation? Exercise? Getting a massage (sign me up!)? Is it taking a nap every day for a month? Is it spending time with your family? Is it crying, screaming, and throwing a tantrum? It sounds weird, but these are the things that we all have to do in order to process emotions. If we don't allow ourselves time to really feel our feelings, then we will just carry around that annoying, exhausting brick backpack for the rest of our lives. No fun. Who wants to ride the bitter and angry train? Nobody.

Now go back up and add, "I have the right to feel my emotions" to your Bill of Rights. Cry when you want to cry, scream when you need to scream, and get the emotions out.

Having said all that, once you process those emotions, you must. Move. FORWARD! Don't allow yourself to stay in those dark places for too long, or you might get stuck. We move forward by getting active. Get up in the morning, get dressed, put on your shoes, brush your hair, call your friends to hang out, go shopping with your mom, go on a picnic with your brother, exercise, cook something delicious, go for a walk, paint your nails, or go visit your grandpa and beat him in a game of pinochle. Move forward.

KEEP YOUR POWER

We are all powerful. We are born with power in us—in our DNA and in our spirits. When we betray our character and integrity, we are giving that power away. It's as if we have a big bowl of Jolly Ranchers (a.k.a. personal power) in our arms, and we are just handing it out. There are many different ways we do this. Here are a few examples . . .

 TOOL #19

Don't Give Your Personal Power Away

- I don't stand up for myself.

- I tell little white lies.

- I don't stand up for my friends.

- I gossip.

- I put myself down to make other people feel better about themselves.

- I participate in activities I don't like just because I want to fit in.

- I hang out with people I don't like just because I want to be popular.

- I don't say "No."

- I procrastinate.

- I bully others through teasing or criticism.

- I don't raise my hand in class, even if I know the answer.

- I follow the crowd.

- I disrespect my parents/guardians/teachers.

- I criticize others.

- I exclude people from the conversation.

- I allow stress to control my mood.

If any of these self-defeating behaviors apply to you, you are giving your power away. That's not a train we want to ride either. Whether you believe it or not, you are powerful. You have so much greatness in you, but when you do these things, you are diminished—you dumb yourself down. If you really want to find out how much magic witch power you have inside of you, you darling Hermione Granger, start working on eliminating these habits from your life. Grab your Elder wand, and get to it.

POWER SCALE

We can gain better perspective on how well we are keeping our power by putting it on a scale.

What kind of scale, Jessie? I'll show you by sharing some examples from my life that I think you will be able empathize with. Watch for these throughout the chapter.

HERE'S A 1 OR 2 ON THE SCALE . . . LYING.

TALES *of* ADVENTURE!

One night, when I was sixteen years old, I was babysitting for my dance teacher. The baby was asleep, and my teacher and her husband were going to be home soon. I thought I would try for a bigger tip by cleaning their home for them. So, I went to the kitchen and scrubbed, washed, sanitized, and organized until the entire room glistened. I finished up by loading the dishwasher, pushing start, and then returned to the family room with a big ole' self-satisfied grin. *Well done, Jessie.*

I was watching TV, when after just a few minutes, I started hearing the faint sounds of Rice Krispies. *What the...? I don't think there should be anything snappin', cracklin', or poppin' in there.* It seems I had used dishwashing SOAP rather than DISHWASHER DETERGENT! There is a difference.

When I got to the kitchen, I encountered about two feet of bubbles covering the entire kitchen floor, and pouring out of the washer! I ran to stop the machine, and then flew to the linen closet to grab as many towels as I could. I busted through that kitchen, slip-sliding all the way. I sopped, dried, and managed to get it all wiped up, tossed the towels in the dryer, and sprinted back to the couch just moments before they walked through the front door. Whew! I tell you what—that floor shined!

After greeting them, I quickly grabbed my things, trying to make a break for it. But, they caught me before I got out the door. "Wow, Jessie, the kitchen is so sparkly!"

I smiled nervously. "Aw, shucks," I replied, still inching toward the door.

Just as I reached it, my teacher walked past the laundry room. "What's in the dryer?" I closed my eyes and said nothing. "What are these towels doing in the dryer, Jessie?"

I slowly turned around, looked her square in the eye, and shrugged, "I don't know." Open. Slam. Jessie bolts for her car.

We are still friends, and to this day, they still don't know why those towels were in the dryer. Actually, who am I kidding? They would have eventually had to open up and turn on their dishwasher, which would scream the tale of what had gone on. Why did I lie? If I had simply told her the TRUTH, she would have laughed her patooty off and said, "Awwww, sweet Jessie. At least you get bonus points just for trying to be nice."

So why did I lie? For some reason, I thought it would be easier to lie and give my power away. Can you relate? Are there things you do that go against your character and compromise your integrity? Humans are weird, aren't we? Why do we do things that make our lives harder and more complicated? Let's stop. That's my vote. Start by making the decision to keep your power. It's amazing how liberating it is to keep your power—to own it!

REMOVE THE BULLY FACTOR

THIS IS ABOUT A 3 OR 4 ON THE PERSONAL POWER SCALE.

Have you ever been bullied? And I don't necessarily mean the, "Meet me by the flagpole after school, punk!" kind of bullying. I mean have you ever had an untrue rumor spread about you? Have you ever been cruelly gossiped about? Have you ever had someone send you a vicious text? Have you ever had someone trip you or bump into you on purpose in the hall? Have you ever been laughed at? Basically, have you ever had your feelings intentionally hurt by another human? If so, then you have been bullied. That's right; even if the person doing the hurting isn't a tough guy wanting to pound your face at lunch, you've been bullied.

Now for a harder question . . .

HAVE YOU EVER *BEEN* A BULLY?

I imagine some of you can come clean and admit that you have teased or gossiped or made fun of someone, and I'm pretty sure if you just beat someone up yesterday, you're aware of the fact that you are, indeed, a bully. But for the rest of you, you might be saying, "Of course not!"

I admit that I was a bully as a teen. Let me tell you, being a bully sucks. Let's just not do it . . . okay?

Take this little quiz to find out if you are a bully.

QUIZ: ARE YOU A BULLY?

Do you rejoice merrily when your enemy fails, gets embarrassed, or gets hurt?

Do you gossip, tease, or make fun of people?

Do you stand by passively watching someone get hurt or ridiculed, without taking a stand for that person?

Do you send cruel text messages?

Do you intentionally leave someone out of certain activities to hurt their feelings?

Do you intentionally avoid certain people just because you don't want to interact with them? (Unless they're toxic—those people you have permission to avoid.)

Do you think you're better than someone else? Prettier, more talented, smarter, cooler, richer, more popular?

Do you enjoy getting someone in trouble—taunting them to do drugs, have sex, pick on someone else, steal?

So, are YOU a bully? Even if just one of these items applies to you, I'm sorry to say that you are. Maybe you were already aware of it, but maybe you were not aware. Whichever applies, do you like that about yourself? Is that how you want to live? How you want to be remembered? Do you enjoy the feeling of hatred that permeates homes, schools, and streets in our communities—in our world? What good does it do? What harm does it do? You already know the answer. I pray and plead with everything in me that you will feel the need to change. If you're spending your time and energy being cruel to other people, you will never become everything you were meant to become. Think of all the time you'll save by choosing to be nice. The fact of the matter is that it has to start—and stop—with YOU! And ME . . . and ALL of us—making a choice to stop hating.

In the video for this chapter, I have included a segment of my speech I give in high schools all around the U.S. It shows exactly what this next tool looks like in real life. Watch the video so we are on the same page as you read this next section.

If you sincerely feel that you are not a bully, but you know for sure you are a victim, or maybe you have realized that you are a little bit of both—what do you do? How do you stop being a target for bullies? How do you stop being a bully? Here is the answer:

LOVE

Love is what every single one of us can do to stop the hatred and change our world. If you don't have love for yourself and others—you won't be happy. Let's forgive the bullies, and forgive yourself for being a bully, and move forward.

If you are a victim of hatred, forgiveness can only take you so far. Here is a little tool that could turn you into someone as powerful as my fave Harry Potter character . . . Luna Lovegood.

It's called . . . (insert *Mission Impossible* theme song)

🔩 TOOL #20

THE C.L.A.W.—YOUR WEAPON OF DIFFUSION

C—Calm

L—Love

A—Avoid

W—Win

That's right, baby. The Claw! Sounds fearsome and, oh, so hip, right? Go with me on this—it works. Just give this section a chance, and I will prove it to you. You can DIFFUSE a bullying situation if you stay CALM, show LOVE and AVOID the bully. Then you WIN!

This weapon works because it diffuses the bully's power. Diffusion means to take the intensity, craziness, hate, anger, and power out of the situation. Like diffusing a bomb . . . but in this case, it's a bully bomb.

And if this sounds like something you've heard before, I don't know, say, the Golden Rule? That's exactly what this is based on. 😊 Do unto others as you would have done unto you!

The golden rule is ancient, timeless, and pure genius. Obviously, it is trying to teach us to be kind to other people, but I think it's even deeper than that. I believe that it gives us a tool to help us deal with difficult people. How, you ask? Here's my theory—it is very, very, very hard to be mean to someone who is being nice to you. Let me say that again. It's very, very, very hard to be MEAN to someone who is being NICE to you. So, if you are dealing with a difficult person and you choose to stay calm and be kind, they will have a hard time trying to be mean.

What do you have to lose? Try the CLAW. The next time someone is saying something creepy, respond with a compliment and just enjoy the confused look on their face. You will win!

Re-cap: The C.L.A.W—Your Weapon of Diffusion

1   Stay CALM, instead of reacting with anger, frustration, and sadness. Getting angry just feeds the fire, and you will continue to be a target and a victim. The reaction is what the bullies want. Don't play into their game. You're stronger than that.

2   Show some kind of LOVE toward the bullies. Compliment them with only one small compliment, and then walk away immediately! If you just ignore it, they will keep pushing and targeting you. You have to "fight" back with a little love in order to take the fun out of the game.

3   AVOID them. This sounds harsh, but bullies are toxic people, and if you try to befriend them, it gives them some power back, and you might get pulled down and bullied again.

4   WIN! By diffusing the situation instead of fueling it, you walk away with the power.

One last thing about bullies—and this is important. If you or someone you know is being hurt by a bully, get help. Your parents, guardians, school counselor, neighbor, administration at your school, basically any trusted adult can help you get the meanness to stop. Don't put up with any type of abuse. You are worth protecting.

Now, let's get back to understanding that scale of personal power.

MANAGING YOUR STRESS

5 OR 6 ON THE SCALE . . . SELF-DESTRUCTION.

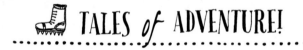

TALES *of* ADVENTURE!

Once upon a time, a few Novembers ago, I went to the kitchen and poured myself a bowl of my favorite cereal: Reese's Puffs, the least healthy cereal you can possibly buy and totally worth every thousand-calorie bite! I carefully prepared this manna from heaven, but before I could take a bite, my little shoulder devil showed up and started telling me: *Why are you eating that, Jessie, you really shouldn't because you're gonna get fat, and you're already pretty chubby!*

Now, we have to back up a little bit. This particular day marked the end of a very stressful three months of my life. I was stressed out all the time, I was completely exhausted, I was way too busy and overscheduled, and I was obsessed with trying to be perfect all the time.

Nobody has it all together all the time. Nobody!

So, my little shoulder devil is telling me that I do not deserve to have a little late night snack. I'm not sure what it was about that moment, but it was the straw that broke my worn out camel's back. I completely lost my mind! I started screaming out loud—as loud as I possibly could—at absolutely no one! If my neighbors had looked in on me through the windows, they would have seen a screaming, crazed madwoman with flailing arms and would have called the insane asylum. I literally lost my mind. I was screaming things like, "I can eat this cereal if I want to," and "I deserve to have a freaking bowl of cereal if I so please!" And, "Who the #$%^@ are you to tell me what I can and cannot eat?" After about a twenty-minute rant, I yelled out one last thing: "I WILL NOT BE AFRAID ANYMORE!"

I laid down on my dirty kitchen floor and sobbed my eyes out. Doesn't it feel so wonderful to have a good cry . . . the ugly cry where snot is everywhere, your mascara is covering your face, and you're hyperventilating—that kind of a really good cry.

I finally sat up, took a deep breath, and thought, *Did I just have a seizure?* And then I thought about what just happened, and it literally was like I had an out-of-body experience because my mind did not seem very present during this epileptic fit. I thought really hard about the last thing I yelled out: *I will not be afraid anymore!* I realized that I was living my life in total fear. I was so afraid of not being perfect, I was so afraid of disappointing people around me by not being perfect, and I was so exhausted because I was constantly putting up the front that I was perfect.

Being a perfectionist will only lead to the loony bin and a pretty padded room, ladies.

I believe that we must allow ourselves to let our guard down. We must allow ourselves to be real and vulnerable and relaxed about life because I know from experience that if you put too much on your plate and try too hard to have it all together—you will absolutely fail.

Bill Cosby said, "I'm not sure what the secret to success is, but I know the quickest way to failure is trying to please everybody." I think that's true, and I sincerely try to live by that now. Here are some stress management techniques that have really helped me. I know they can help you have a more balanced life. Keeping your power means you must find the balance in your schedule and what you expect of yourself.

REMEMBER THAT CHAT ABOUT SELF-CARE, *BLINKIN WINKIN*!!?

TOOL #21

STRESS MANAGEMENT

Stress is ever present in your teen years. Teens have a lot to balance with school, homework, extracurricular activities, family, internships, preparing for college, social life, etc. Whew! It stresses me out just thinking about it.

Seventeen Magazine shares some great anti-stress tips from real girls:

The Perfect Tune: *"I find playing my guitar and writing a song or listening to some of my favorite songs or artists on replay is very relaxing."*

—**MICHELLE, 16, VOORHEES, NJ**

Girls' Night In: *"I call up my best friend, and we have a lazy day by getting in our PJs and lounging around, watching Mary-Kate and Ashley movies while eating cake icing. It helps so much!"*

—**BRITTANY, 17, KNOXVILLE, TN**

A Breath of Fresh Air: *"I always go for a one-hour walk every day after school. It keeps my mind clear, and I get tons of fresh air!"*

—**HAILEY, 15, FRIENDSWOOD, TX**

Talk It Out: *"If something's really stressful, I talk to my mom or my friends about it. I know they can't always fix the problem, but sometimes just talking to someone helps."*

—**FIONA, 16, DUNROBIN, ONTARIO, CANADA**

Feel the Burn: *"I tend to get really worked up about small things like work, friends, school, and family. When this happens, I vent and take it out on whoever is near me and—as* *a result—end up hurting my friends and family. To relieve stress, I crank up my iPod and go for a run or do as many sit-ups as I can until I'm exhausted. Exercise raises endorphins (which make you feel good!) and helps circulation. So, by doing something physical, I take something that is bad for me (and those around me) and turn it into something beneficial."*

—**AILISH, 17, GUELPH, ONTARIO, CANADA**

Aromatherapy: *"It may sound weird, but I spray on my favorite perfume when I'm stressed. Victoria Secret's Coconut Passion helps me relax from school, homework, clubs, and sports."*

—**JESS, 16, CANTON, MA**

Alone Time: *"Sometimes I need a day off from the usual craziness, so I spend a day with myself. I turn on my favorite songs, paint my nails, or read a book I've been too busy to read."*

—**CALLIE, 14, INVER GROVE HEIGHTS, MN**

Journaling: *"I always have to get out how I feel. If I can't talk to someone directly, I write it down. My journal has always been my de-stressing savior!"*

—**SUZANNE, 17, TORONTO, ONTARIO, CANADA**

Yoga: *"After a long week at work and studying, I like to do yoga to unwind. It helps, especially the breathing exercises."*

—**CELESTE, 19, MIAMI, FL**[1]

Let's recap and add a few ideas for managing stress:

- Music

- Girls' night

- Take a walk

- Talk to a trusted friend

- Exercise

- Aromatherapy

- Alone time

- Journaling

- Yoga

- Laugh

- Hot bath

- Deep Breathing

- Cook something yummy and healthy

- Massage

- Nap

- Slide and swing at a playground

✐ JOURNAL TIME

Take a moment, get that fuzzy feather pen, and jot down some ideas.

What do you usually do when you're stressed? How do you want to deal with stress?

_____

_____

_____

_____

_____

_____

_____

_____

_____

_____

_____

_____

_____

_____

Now, back to the personal power scale.

STEER CLEAR OF TOXIC RELATIONSHIPS

7 OR 8 ON THE SCALE . . . INNOCENTLY FINDING YOURSELF IN A BAD SITUATION.

This requires a lot of power, but you can find the strength to get out.

🥾 TALES of ADVENTURE!

When I was a naïve twelve-year-old, my friend and I were hired by her family friend to paint his new condo. It was a great job that paid us really well. I got to spend a few hours with my friend every day. We talked and talked and talked and had a blast. The family friend that had hired us was nice, gave us great tips, made sure that we always had yummy things to eat, and that we had music playing. Yet, from the very beginning, something felt very off. I couldn't put my finger on it, but I didn't really like being around him.

On the second to last night of our job, he invited us to swim in his hot tub. We had brought our swimming suits and were way excited. We thought we were by ourselves, but all of a sudden, the guy showed up with some movies and asked us if we wanted some entertainment.

We said, "Sure."

He asked, "How about a cartoon?" He proceeded to put in an anime cartoon that was completely pornographic. I felt so uncomfortable and didn't know how to handle it, because I had never been in a situation like that before.

After a little while, the guy came back into the room and said, "Do you like the video?" She and I both looked at each other with perplexed facial expressions thinking, *How on earth could he think that we like this?*

Then he asked us if he could get in the hot tub with us.

My friend immediately said, "Okay." This was, after all, a close family friend who was trusted by her family.

I, however, was horrified by the idea and instantly wanted to get out of that hot tub, get out of that house, and never come back. He took off his shirt right in front of us, dropped his pants revealing a swimming suit underneath, and got into the hot tub. I absolutely couldn't stand it, so I instantly got out.

I never went back to finish the painting job, and I didn't care.

There are two lessons here. First, trust your intuition. I knew at the very beginning of starting to work for this man that something was a little off. I wasn't sure what it was, but I didn't feel comfortable around him from the get-go. Trust your instincts. That beautiful little Jiminy Cricket we're all born with is a smart fella.

Second, he was "priming" us. This is the actual technical term that law enforcement people use when they are talking about sexual predators and their prey (a.k.a. innocent girls like me). Predators start out being really nice and fun, and making sure they win your trust. Then they push the envelope just a little—in my case, putting on that pornographic cartoon. They wait to see what the reaction is and make their move.

Becoming more aware of how predators think can arm you with the knowledge you need to avoid situations like this in the first place AND to help your friends avoid them, too. My only real regret with this whole experience is that I didn't do everything I could to get my friend out of danger, too. I should have talked to her about it and told her not to go back. We should have talked to her parents about it too, but we didn't; we stayed silent. Don't be silent girls—speak up!

Moving right along . . . last example of our scale.

9 OR 10 ON THE PERSONAL POWER PAIN SCALE . . . TOXIC RELATIONSHIPS.

 IF YOU HAVEN'T WATCHED THE VIDEO FOR THIS CHAPTER, GET ON IT, *BANDAID BUGGY!*

TALES *of* ADVENTURE!

When I was in college, I met this guy. I was immediately crazy about him because he was so fun. You have probably guessed that I have a "yellow" personality, which means I'm always interested in a good time. And HE was a good time! He made me laugh and was so spontaneous, but best of all—he was crazy about me. On one of our first dates, we were starving, but didn't have even fifteen cents between us. Next thing I know, we're playing a crazy game rushing from one apartment door to another totally out of breath and in a huge hurry.

"Hey! (Pant, pant, enormous smiles) We're on a Scavenger Hunt, (rasping breaths) and all we have left to find is a red safety pin or a dollar! (Breathe, pant) Can you help us out?"

Well, of course, nobody had a red safety pin—I don't think they even make such a thing. So what did they give us? That's right. We ended up with twenty bucks, and scarfed down a Blondie from Applebees. BEST. TIME. EVER! That was this guy, in a nutshell. And I was mad about him!

But after a while, I started to notice some things that really bothered me. One night, we were out to dinner, and I had just bought an adorable navy blue shirt with a boat-scoop neckline which showed off my best feature—my clavicles. Calm down, they're just collar bones. He looked me up and down, and curtly said, "Jessie, I don't think blue is your color." OUCH! That little comment crushed me because I had just bought that shirt and thought I looked fabulous: like a little Audrey Hepburn! And I *did* think blue was my color.

Here's the interesting part though. What was my response? Well, what I MEANT to say was, "Umm, hello? Do you really think you get to tell me what colors I should or shouldn't wear? I'll be the one to decide what's right or wrong for me! Mmmmm-hmmmm!" (Three attitude snaps in a "Z" formation.)

Did I have the confidence to say that? No. What I actually said was, "Oh, you don't like it? I thought you would!" And regrettably, the next time we had a date, I went to my closet and passed right over the blue shirt. Because it "wasn't my color." Not cool. It makes me cringe that I chose not to stand up for myself—that I just took his criticism and gave my power away. I cringe even more to realize that was the first red flag of many that I was in a toxic relationship. I opened the door wide spankin' open for him to use and abuse me. I allowed it by not valuing myself enough to stand up for myself. Confidence . . . such an important thing!

He was testing the waters that night to see how I would respond, and I did just as he wanted me to. I withered and died . . . just a little, because it wasn't like he slapped me in the face or anything too extreme. But just that fast, the situation started to become abusive. He started ordering me around like a slave, manipulating me into doing homework for him, cleaning up after him, washing his clothes for him, and even more annoying things. He also tried to control my schedule. He wanted me to call him right after school every day, and if I didn't, he would tease me, saying things like, "Why didn't you call me—were you out cheating on me?" Or he would manipulate me by saying things like, "I just missed you so much. I can't see straight unless I know you're okay." Gag. That's called manipulation, and girls, we are just as capable of it as guys are.

See through this kind of garbage! It's a twisted, toxic game, and it is a very real game. It still hurts me to think about how far I allowed it to be played. I was with this jerk for an entire year of my life. He criticized, manipulated, controlled, and coerced me into sexual activities that I didn't want to participate in, but did anyway because I didn't have these tools. I didn't have the confidence to say, "UMM, NO! GET OUT OF MY LIFE!" Did I mention this was college? I was supposed to be mature enough to take control of my life, but I wasn't.

That is why I choose to talk about it now. That is why I choose to do something about it today. I am doing my best to warn you of the dangers of abuse. This is how I find healing from what I've been through. This is so important and MUST be talked about. We can prevent dating violence!

The saddest part here is that my story is totally common. Check out these stats from WomensIssues.about.com[2]:

- Each year, approximately one in four adolescent's reports verbal, physical, emotional, or sexual abuse.

- Approximately one in five adolescents reports being a victim of emotional abuse.

- Approximately one in five high school girls has been physically or sexually abused by a dating partner.

- Dating violence among their peers is reported by 54 percent of high school students.

- One in three teens report knowing a friend or peer who has been physically hurt by his or her partner through violent actions which included hitting, punching, kicking, slapping, and/or choking.

- 80 percent of teens believe verbal abuse is a serious issue for their age group.

- Nearly 80 percent of girls who have been victims of physical abuse in their dating relationships continue to date the abuser.

- Nearly 20 percent of teen girls who have been in a relationship said that their boyfriend had threatened violence or self-harm in the event of a break-up.

- Nearly 70 percent of young women who have been raped knew their rapist; the perpetrator was or had been a boyfriend, friend, or casual acquaintance.

- The majority of teen dating abuse occurs in the home of one of the partners.

According to an article from Princeton University, teens are going through so many changes, physically and mentally, that they are actually prone to having self-esteem challenges:

Some researchers believe that it is the combination of so many changes occurring simultaneously that makes early adolescence problematic for many young people. Coping with the stresses of pubertal change, school transitions, cognitive development, and the dynamics of dating at the same time puts young adolescents at risk for developmental problems such as lowered self-esteem and early sexual activity.[3]

HOW DO YOU THINK ABUSE STARTS?

If a couple are out on their very first date, and suddenly, the girl just hauls off and slaps the guy across the face for not ordering her the right food, do you think he'll stay calm, sit back, and enjoy the rest of the date? Of course not. But, what if she is so sweet and fun at first, then she casually criticizes his shirt; then, on the next date, she calls him a dork for the way he laughs, but says she was "just kidding." Then, a couple weeks down the road, she makes fun of him for missing a couple shots at his basketball game. Then, she tells him she can't stand his friends and expects him to cancel plans to be with her . . . and only with her. And finally, the day comes that she smacks him while they're having a disagreement. Now, can you see it? Abuse, whether it is verbal, emotional, physical, sexual, or mental, always starts with smaller forms of cruelty.

Criticism, teasing, taunting, bullying, manipulation, and controlling behaviors are all huge red flags signaling worse things to come. The calm before the storm. Just to clarify, I'm not saying that if you are on a date with a boy and he tells you blue isn't your color that he is going to become physically abusive toward you. Maybe he won't. But the fact of the matter is **maybe he will**. And even if he never hits you, why would you want to be with someone who sees nothing wrong with tearing you down and making you feel worthless?

Never allow yourself to be treated this way. YOU DESERVE TO BE TREATED LIKE ROYALTY!

LEARN TO RECOGNIZE TOXIC RELATIONSHIPS.

Take a look at this quiz to know if your boyfriend, friend, even a family member is an abuser, in any form. You must know what the warning signs are so you can identify current toxic relationships you might need to sever or get help with. If you can't remove a toxic person from your social circle, create healthy boundaries to keep their toxicity in check. Remember, the goal here is to prevent a toxic relationship from forming in the first place.

QUIZ: RED FLAGS OF ABUSE

Do they have a temper?

Do they put you down and make you feel bad about yourself?

Do they scream at you and then the next day bring you chocolates and say they're "so sorry" and "it will never happen again."

Do they try to control who you hang out with, where you go, how you dress, and more?

Do they hurt you physically—squeezing your hand, pushing you, hitting you, poking you, shoving you?

Do they tease you about being fat/ugly/annoying? And then say, "Just kidding." Or "Take a joke!"?

How do you feel when you're around them? Anxious, worried, scared, feeling like you have to walk on eggshells?

Do they put pressure on you to be physically intimate and then put you down if you are hesitant?

Do they threaten you, saying they will hurt you if you ever break up or tattle tale on them?

If even one or two of these items fits your relationship—
get out now and stay out! Did I mention that you are worth a
healthy, loving, safe relationship? Well, you are.

HOW DO YOU GET OUT?

The best way I know of to avoid, or get out of, toxic relationships
is by having the strength and confidence to say, "NO." If you go
out on a date with someone who shows even a glimpse of controlling or manipulative tendencies—or maybe you just know
you aren't interested in a second date, don't hesitate to say, "No."

If you are hanging out with someone who is critical of you,
and you just don't like being around their negative energy, the
next time they want to hang out, kindly say, "No thanks." Period.
No excuses. No justifying. No lies about how you have to floss
your cat. Just say "No." That is a complete sentence. Remember
tool #3? Flip back to Skill #1 and review some ways to say no if
you find this is hard for you. Give yourself permission to say,
"No." And if it hurts their feelings? Well, bless their hearts, they
can just deal with it. Too harsh? No ma'am, I'm still right. That's
how much I love you. I'm willing to tell the harsh truths.

You don't have to explain, justify, or make any excuse. When
the toxic person wants to hang out, you say, "No."

You must sever the connection from the toxic relationship
BEFORE it becomes scary, as well as learn how to avoid toxic relationships in the first place. Begin by following your instincts.
If you are with someone, and you feel worried, nervous, in-
timidated, or vulnerable—respect those feelings, and remove

yourself from the situation. Let me perfectly clear—if you are in a relationship with someone, whether a boy or girl, whether romantic or just a friend you hang out with, you have permission to break up or stop hanging out with him/her if he/she is abusive. Harsh right? Yep—that's exactly how I intend it to be. You are worth protecting!

If you find yourself already in a bad situation with someone who is controlling, mean, and manipulative, there is help. If you don't know what to do or how to get out of the relationship, go see your school counselor or your parents or your best friend's mom. They can help! You might think it's lame or weak . . . that you ought to be able to figure it out yourself . . . that it isn't so bad . . . that you can handle it on your own. But chances are you could use some assistance. Ask. For. HELP! And if you're hesitant because you're scared the person you're trying to get away from will get mad . . . yeah, ESPECIALLY THEN, get help!

In order to live your life, you must feel safe and confident, not scared and controlled. Girl or guy, you can call the domestic violence hotline at 1-800-772-SAFE. You can also visit the National Domestic Violence Hotline website at www.NDVH.org or the National Teen Dating Abuse Hotline at www.LoveIsRespect.org. It's all confidential and anonymous, and they know what they're doing.

If you're feeling embarrassed and destroyed because you think you're the only person this has happened to, you are mistaken. If that were the case, there would be no hotlines or websites dedicated to this problem. The Centers for Disease

Control and Prevention report that "9.4 percent of high school students report being hit, slapped, or physically hurt on purpose by their boyfriend or girlfriend in the twelve months prior to the survey."[4] WHAT? Is that staggering to anyone else? I think it is unacceptable. Do you agree? I knew you would. Please know that you are not alone. There is no excuse for abuse. Help is ready and standing by!

When you are confident with who you are, and know that you deserve love and respect, then you will get it. You won't settle for someone who is nice "most of the time." You will know that you are entitled to a solid, healthy relationship that will take you where you want to go in your life. And when you are confident, you can avoid abusive situations so much easier.

WHEN A LADY MAKES THE CHOICE TO KEEP HER POWER, THAT IS WHEN SHE CAN TRULY SHINE.

 **CHALLENGE**

This week, evaluate your relationships: friends, family, boyfriends. Is there any relationship that needs to be cleaned up? Meaning: are there things that have been bugging you for a while that need to be addressed and dealt with? Are there certain people that just need to not be on your iPhone favorites anymore? Take a step back, look around, and pay attention to how you feel when you think about certain humans. If you need to create stronger boundaries or remove someone from your life altogether, so be it. It has to be done so you can have the life you were meant for. You can always be kind, tactful, and honest while setting firm rules for respect in your life.

Leaders choose to never allow toxic people to hold them back . . . it all comes down to our choices.

WRITE ABOUT YOUR EXPERIENCE:

_____

_____

_____

SELF-RESPECT

> ## "Self-Respect is the cornerstone of all virtue."

—CONFUCIUS

The funniest question I've ever been asked is . . . "Are your legs different lengths?" True story. Apparently, when I walk I look like Tiny Tim and Tyra Banks having a hoedown. Why someone would allow words like that to escape their mouth is beyond me, although I have been known to ask women when they're due to have a baby only to discover, to my horror, that they're not pregnant. So I'm not one to talk. (LIFE RULE: never ever, EVER, under any circumstances, ask a woman if she is pregnant—even if she looks like she's carrying Hagrid and every single one of the Weasley children in her belly . . . don't ask!)

The point? It's impossible to please everyone. No matter how much we spend on the latest and greatest makeup, designer jeans, hair gel, styling wands, or, in my case, a new leg, there will always be someone who doesn't approve of your look, your style, or you for that matter. So, forget them! Repeat after me: "Not everyone has to like me. Not everyone has to like me. Not everyone has to like me. Not everyone has to like me . . . " That's your new mantra.

Respecting ourselves enough to put ourselves together simply means that we are clean, our clothes are in good, functioning order, and we take time to do our hair and makeup. While you're thinking about what that means for you, here's a scenario to show why this is so important.

 PAY ATTENTION *PONCHO PIE TRUCK*.

Two girls go in for a job interview. The first, let's call her Rosie, is very put together. She has very basic, yet lovely makeup on. Her hair is clean and curled, and her clothes are clean and neatly pressed. She also smells delectable. She aces the interview because she is completely qualified and very intelligent.

The second girl, let's call her Carlotta, rolls out of bed, throws on some gym pants and some old sneakers, throws her hair up in a ponytail, doesn't bother with any makeup, and smells like she . . . just rolled out of bed. She goes into the interview and totally aces it because she is also completely qualified and very intelligent.

Which girl gets the job?

I know it sounds shallow, but of course it is the girl who is put together. Do you know why? It is because she has shown her boss that she has respect for herself, and by showing him that she has respect for herself, the boss knows that she will have respect for him and for the company. Grooming and hygiene habits are much more about respect than beauty.

SELF-RESPECT

Notice how this chapter is titled "Self-Respect," not "Beauty"?

Self-respect is about putting your best foot forward. It is also a lovely source of CONFIDENCE, and that is a huge part of what ladyhood is all about. The goal here is for you to realize that you have a lot of control over how people receive you. If you want that job, respect yourself enough to put yourself together for the interview. If you want your teachers to respect you, show them you respect yourself first by coming to class rested, clean, and ready to learn. If you want that guy to notice you, make sure you take the time to brush your hair and smell good.

How we dress and how we carry ourselves is a form of communication. It is part of our non-verbal communication. What is your nonverbal communication communicating to those around you? Do people think that you have respect for yourself and for them just by looking at you, or is there some work needing to be done there?

 # TOOL #22

Hygiene Checklist (circle one)

Do you shower daily?

YES   NO   SOMETIMES

Do you use soap between your toes, in your belly button, private places, behind your ears, underarms, bottom of your feet?

YES   NO   SOMETIMES

Do you put on deodorant every morning?

YES   NO   SOMETIMES

Do you clean your ears every day?

YES   NO   SOMETIMES

Do you wash your face before bed?

YES   NO   SOMETIMES

Do you wash your hands after using the ladies room?

YES   NO   SOMETIMES

Do you trim your eyebrows?

YES   NO   SOMETIMES

Do you brush your teeth morning and night?

    YES   NO   SOMETIMES

Do you floss daily?

    YES   NO   SOMETIMES

Do you trim your finger and toenails?

    YES   NO   SOMETIMES

Do you get eight hours of sleep at night?

    YES   NO   SOMETIMES

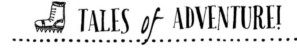

TALES *of* ADVENTURE!

WHAT IS A Q-TIP?

I grew up a complete disaster. (My sweet parents both worked full-time, and after their divorce, they were both in survival mode. They weren't capable of functioning at optimal levels. It is important for me to say that so you don't judge them. I absolutely adore my parents, and I know they did the best job they could.) No one taught me the importance of trimmed nails or having sparkling clean ears.

This is so embarrassing, but I honestly didn't use Q-tips to clean my ears regularly until I got married. I watched my husband use them every single day, and I thought, *Wow, maybe I should do that.* (I seriously didn't admit that to him until just now—as I'm writing this . . . nine years of marriage later. He's rolling his eyes at me while shaking his head.) My husband has impeccable hygiene habits—which is something I completely love about him! It's so attractive that he always smells like heaven and is always totally put together. He's such a hunk of burnin' love . . . now I want to kiss him—right this second. Maybe I will . . . Focus, Jessie!

NOT POLISHED?

Okay, let's take a look at a life-changing moment from when I was fourteen. I was riding in the car with my singing manager. She was trying to work a deal with the State Fair director to get me a slot singing on their stage that summer. I really wanted the gig because I would actually get paid, and they would give me free funnel cakes. 😊 I was sitting there in the passenger seat listening to my manager talk on the phone when I vividly heard the woman on the line say, "I've seen Jessie perform before, and she is not that polished." I didn't get the gig. I was crushed. I had no idea I wasn't a "polished" performer. The awesome news was that NOW I KNEW! From then on, I worked harder to refine my performing skills, I worked harder at showing up for my gigs one hundred percent prepared, one hundred percent ready, one hundred percent put together. My work paid off. The very next summer, I was headlining not one but TWO shows at the state fair.

That should give you an idea of what a mess I was as a teen. Therefore, I am in the unique position of being very qualified to teach this stuff because you know I don't say any of this from a judgmental pedestal. I know exactly what it's like to have to LEARN this stuff.

Sometimes the truth hurts, but we can choose to let it hurt us or teach us. I am thankful that I have that woman's voice in my head telling me I wasn't polished, because it fuels me to work hard to become my very best self. I promise this is an important lesson for all of us. Showing up in our lives being put together and respectful of ourselves can only be a positive thing for you.

The Centre for Adolescent Health says:

Keeping clean is an important part of staying healthy. For example, the simple act of washing hands before eating and after using the toilet is a proven and effective tool for fighting off germs and avoiding sickness. Being clean and well-presented is also an important part of confidence for teenagers. If your child's body and breath smell OK, his clothes are clean, and he's on top of his basic personal hygiene, it can help him fit in with other people.[1]

Tell me if you can relate to this story: It's the first day of school; you spent an hour getting ready. You had your outfit picked out a week in advance, and you are ready to make a dazzling first impression. You make it through the whole first half of the day without catastrophe, then the nightmare you dread actually occurs. You're sitting at lunch and your friend accidently drops her entire tray of food onto your cream-colored sundress. Ketchup from the hamburger, diet coke, ranch from her salad . . . all over your adorable ensemble. This may or may not be a true story from my life. 😊

What do you do in emergencies? Even the less dramatic emergencies call for pre-planning. In your rush to get out the door for school, you forget deodorant . . . wouldn't it be great if you had an extra stick in your car? Your bangs are just not staying out of your eyes, and they are driving you nuts . . . wouldn't it be great if you just happened to have a travel-size hairspray bottle in your backpack? A button on your shirt pops off in the middle of English, and there's a clear shot to your undergarments . . . wouldn't it be great to have a mini sewing kit in your locker? (Assuming you know how to sew on a button, of course.) Or what if your boyfriend surprises you with flowers during math class and it makes you cry? Now you have mascara all over your cute face, and you need to freshen up. Having some basic make-up with you can save the day.

See what I mean? I'm sure you've been there, just like I have. Taking some time to go to the dollar store and pick up some items for your own personal emergency hygiene kit could really be a life-saver when it comes to good grooming practices.

EMERGENCY HYGIENE KIT

I recommend having an emergency hygiene kit in your car at all times—if you don't drive yet, put it in the family car or in your backpack.

THE MUST-HAVES:

- Deodorant (one that won't melt in your car)

- Q-tips

- Hairspray

- Brush and comb

- Basic makeup: mascara, lip gloss, concealer, powder (no one likes a shiny nose)

- Small spray bottle of water for wrinkled shirts (the most ingenious way to iron. Spray your shirt down while you're wearing it and just smooth the wrinkles out. You'll be dry within minutes, and the wrinkles will disappear!)

- Perfume or body spray (Dollar stores have the best body sprays ever! They are tiny, cheap, and smell heavenly.)

- Clear nail polish (Not only will they give your nails a quick beauty boost, but they will also stop runs in tights and hose.)

- Gum or Tic-tacs for a quick breath freshener

- Travel-size sewing kit: just in case you lose a button on your shirt

- Tide-to-Go or a bleach pen . . . when spaghetti sauce meets your white cami

- A change of clothes—you just never know!

- Band-Aids

- Tylenol for the inconvenient headache

- Tampons and pads

- Handheld mirror

Now that you are ready for that unexpected disaster, don't you feel oh-so-much more confident? You do? Excellent . . . I'm doing my job.

We are all at different places in what we feel we need to do to care for ourselves. Consider these levels of loveliness, and think about where you are and what feels right to you.

HYGEINE LEVELS OF LOVELINESS

LEVEL 1: THE BASICS

- Showering Daily

- Cleaning ears with Q-tips (Just the outer part ladies— don't swab in your ear canal.)

- Trimming finger and toenails so there are no chips or hangnails

- Putting on deodorant every morning

- Washing hands after using the restroom and before handling food

- Washing your face morning and night, and using a gentle moisturizer afterward

- Using sunscreen to protect your beautiful skin
- Getting eight hours of sleep

LEVEL 2: PAMPER YOURSELF

- After washing your face, use an under-eye moisturizer and a separate moisturizer for the rest of your face. The skin underneath your eyes is very delicate and requires special care. The better you take care of your skin now, the happier you will be as you age.

- After showering, use a good lotion on your whole body. Your skin is your largest organ and needs extra moisture. Make sure you use extra on heels, knees, elbows, and your neck.

- Organic coconut oil is a great deep conditioner. I recommend doing a deep condition on your hair once a week. Leave it on for an hour or so before you shower, and then just wash it out, and shampoo and condition as usual.

- Invest in a good leave-in conditioner for your hair. Your hair will thank you for the extra love!

- File your nails and put one coat of clear nail polish on to strengthen them and give them a lovely shine

- Exfoliate your body daily in the shower with a loofah sponge. Your skin loves getting rid of dead skin that's just hanging out on the surface . . . help it out!

- Exfoliate your face once or twice a week with a facial buff puff pad. Don't push too hard, but give it a good scrub to help get rid of dead skin cells. Your skin will renew itself and give you that angelic glow.

LEVEL 3: GIRLY GIRL

Once you master Levels 1 and 2 of essential hygiene habits, you can move on to this level, but do so realizing that it is just for fun. There are so many teenagers I know who have no desire to apply makeup or braid their hair. To those girls, I say, "Rock on!" I love celebrating natural beauty. At this season of your life, you have the fabulous opportunity to see makeup as a toy. It's something fun to play with, but you certainly won't die without it. If you love makeup and wear it daily, that's fine, too—as long as you don't base your worth on it, and you know you are beautiful without it! Say it with me . . . "I AM BEAUTIFUL . . . WITH OR WITHOUT MAKEUP!"

Here are some things you can do for that special event or to "girl it up":

- Style your hair in creative, unique, fun ways

- Wear makeup, playing with different colors of eye shadow and lipstick

- Paint your nails all sorts of funky shades; check out all the designs and stickers to express yourself.

- YouTube is such a great resource for hair, makeup, and all things—GIRL tutorials. Some of my favorite channels on YouTube for fun girl play-time are:

* Abby Smith's Twist Me Pretty (My BFF!)

* Luxy Hair

* SierraMarieMakeup

* MyLifeAsEva

* Laurensboutique

Take a good look at how you present yourself. Are you repre-
senting yourself accurately? Are people able to see the real you
when they meet you for the first time? Do you want people to see
you as strong, confident, capable, and put together? The truth is
that if we want to make that kind of first impression, we have to
dress accordingly. Take a good, honest look, and decide how you
feel about this whole self-respect topic. Make changes according
to how you feel. If you don't think this whole idea is that big of
a deal . . . you just might change your mind in a few years. Trust
me. Starting now will just give you a leg-up.

RESPECT YOUR STUFF

One last little thing I want to touch on PDQ. Another aspect of
self-respect is how we take care of our stuff. Someone once told
me that how you treat your belongings is how you will treat the
people you love the most. I think that is true in a lot of ways.
Think about it. If you take the time to put your clothes away,
vacuum the carpet, dust your dresser, and organize your jew-
elry, that level of care can teach you how to put effort into the

relationships that matter most. If you are anything like I was, your room might look like Hogwarts Castle after Voldemort's attack.

If it's a mess, ask yourself this question: "Do I treat the most important people in my life the way I treat my room?" Be honest with yourself. If the answer is "no" and you feel you treat your loved ones with kindness and respect, that's awesome! High five and two gold stars for you. If the answer is "yes," you admit you don't treat valuable people with enough respect, just like your stuff, remedy that. Taking care of your room will teach you to be disciplined, and that discipline will strengthen your relationships. I guarantee it. Happy vacuuming. ☺

CONFIDENT, CLASSY LADIES RESPECT THEMSELVES ENOUGH TO PUT THEIR BEST FOOT FORWARD.

CHALLENGE

Take your hygiene to the next level. Decide where you think you are with your level of self-respect, and take one more step up. Learning and living great habits of self-respect now will benefit you and the people around you for years to come!

. . . it all comes down to our choices.

WRITE ABOUT YOUR EXPERIENCE:

_____

_____

_____

_____

_____

_____

_____

_____

_____

_____

_____

_____

GOAL-SETTING

"Do one thing every day that scares you."

—ELEANOR ROOSEVELT

S ince we are talking about goals here, MY goal for you in this chapter is to realize a harsh truth . . . no one is going to hand you success. Your parents can't do your pushups for you; your teachers cannot memorize your times tables for you. You have to do the work if you want to succeed.

Here are four aspects to goal setting that I know will help you in your life!

1   Identify your Identity

2   Dream

3   Focus

4   Use time management skills

Okay, let's hit it!

1. IDENTIFY YOUR IDENTITY:

So, throughout this book we have talked about skills that can seriously help you become a creature of pure awesomeness! Now, it's time to make some decisions about who you are and what you want to become. To own who you are—every sweet aspect of your personality. You are completely unique and amazing. Never hide who you are or try to change to please someone. Understand you must know who you are before you can truly decide where you want to go—or what goals are important to you. Let's explore this identity thing.

HERE ARE SOME FUNKY FACTS ABOUT ME—A LITTLE GLIMPSE INTO MY UNIVERSE:

- I am a lousy cook.
- I love recycling.
- I'm afraid of the dark.
- I hate it when people are mean to animals.
- I love America—I am a proud patriot.
- My pogo-stick jumping skills are dazzling.
- I am a fun mom. (Hide-and-seek at my house is an experience!)
- I love old Jazz music and black-and-white movies from the '20s and '30s.

- My favorite animals are the manatee and English bulldogs.

- My favorite food is alfredo sauce with bread sticks . . . mmmmm!

- Child abuse hurts my heart.

- I collect those smashed, oval penny coins you see at amusement parks.

- I love to dream.

- I get a kick out of making people laugh and think.

- And my sincerest desire is to make a difference in the world and leave a positive legacy.

These are just some of the things that make me unique and important. There are so many more little facets that make up who I am, but these are a few important parts of me.

You can't set effective goals unless you have seriously pinned down your identity. Don't worry, though; the cool thing about an identity is that it can change, grow, and progress over time.

TOOL #23

The Point of YOU . . . Identity

So, who are you? Here are more questions than you could ever want or need to help you answer that and get you going on your journey to authentic self-discovery.

✏ JOURNAL TIME

Go get your favorite bedazzled writing utensil, and buckle up. ☺

QUESTIONS AND MORE QUESTIONS

Things you rock! What do you love about yourself, and what are you awesome at?

_____

_____

_____

_____

_____

Things you don't rock so much. Let's cut to the chase . . . what sucks in your life, and what do you suck at doing?

_____

_____

_____

_____

_____

If you could have an endless supply of any food, what would you get?

_____

_____

_____

If you were an animal, what would you be, and why?

_____

_____

_____

What is one goal you'd like to accomplish during your lifetime?

_____

_____

_____

When you were little, who was your favorite superhero, and why?

_____

_____

_____

What's your favorite thing to do in the summer?

_____

_____

_____

If they made a movie of your life, what would it be about, and which actor would you want to play you?

_____

_____

_____

If you were an ice cream flavor, which one would you be, and why?

_____

_____

_____

What makes you sad?

_____

_____

_____

_____

What makes you angry?

_____

_____

_____

What's your favorite cartoon character, and why?

_____

_____

_____

If you could visit any place in the world, where would you choose to go and why?

_____

_____

_____

If you had a million dollars and knew all the right people and had all the time in the world, what would you do?

_____

_____

_____

Are you a morning or night person?

_____

_____

_____

What are your favorite hobbies?

_____

_____

_____

_____

What are your pet peeves or interesting things about you that you dislike?

_____

_____

_____

_____

What's the weirdest thing you've ever eaten?

_____

_____

_____

What are your favorite things about each person in your family?

_____

_____

_____

Do you have any unique or quirky habits?

_____

_____

_____

If you had to describe yourself using three words, what would they be?

_____

_____

Who are your heroes? Are there people you look up to that you would like to be like? Are there characteristics in certain people that you want to have?

_____

_____

_____

What excites you?

_____

_____

_____

What goals did you have for yourself as a child?

_____

_____

_____

What do you feel you were meant for? What's your purpose?

_____

_____

_____

_____

Where do you want to be in five or ten years?

_____

_____

_____

_____

What are you afraid of?

_____

_____

_____

What did you wish you had done as a child but didn't?

_____

_____

_____

What is the most important thing you learned in the last year?

_____

_____

_____

What is one piece of advice your parents have given you that you actually use?

_____

_____

_____

What do you like about how your parents/guardians parent/guard you?

_____

_____

_____

What do you procrastinate?

_____

_____

What five things inspire you most?

_____

_____

_____

_____

_____

What is one of your favorite/happiest childhood memories?

_____

_____

_____

FAVORITES—FILL IN!

FOOD:

MOVIE:

HOBBY:

SPORT:

SCENT:

BOOK:

ANIMAL:

PET:

DESSERT:

SONG:

BAND:

STORE:

BRAND:

MAGAZINE:

WEBSITE:

YOUTUBE VIDEO:

SOCIAL MEDIA SITE:

VACATION:

NOW BACK TO SOME DEEP THINKING:

What world wrong would you right?

_____

_____

_____

If you were queen for a day, what law would you pass or change?

_____

_____

_____

What's your favorite place in this world?

_____

_____

_____

If you could make someone vanish, who would it be?

_____

_____

_____

If you die today, who will you miss the most?

_____

_____

_____

What's the movie or book you've watched or read over and over?

_____

_____

_____

What kind of activities do you want to participate in when you're ninety years old?

_____

_____

_____

What would you do if you and your family lost all your money and your home?

_____

_____

_____

_____

What is something you've always wanted to try? Even if it's just once.

_____

_____

_____

Are you a better person today than you were this time last year?

_____

_____

_____

What's your favorite thing to do at home?

_____

_____

_____

If you were in a sinking ship with everyone you know and you could only fit two people in the lifeboat with you, who would you save?

_____

_____

_____

How do people perceive you?

_____

_____

_____

What do you want your legacy to be?

_____

_____

_____

WHO ARE YOU? WHAT DO YOU WANT OUT OF LIFE?

_____

_____

_____

_____

_____

_____

_____

_____

_____

With all of these identity ideas swirling in your head, create a mission statement to match your vision of glory for your world. Just one or two sentences that you can use to motivate yourself to stay on this fast track to awesomeness you just created. Example: Here's mine—*When I'm ninety, sitting in the nursing home eating my Jell-O, I WILL be happy with the choices I made.* Easy breezy. Just something that can be your personal mantra.

MISSION STATEMENT:

_____

_____

_____

_____

_____

_____

_____

_____

2. DREAM

As a singer, I get asked a lot how I got started and what advice I have for teens to get their own music career going. The only wisdom I really have to share on that subject is to just sing! Or play that Kazoo or paint or swim or . . . whatever your art medium is . . . just do it! Sing anywhere, for anyone, anytime. Sing when you're cold, sing when you're sick, sing when you're tired, sing first thing in the morning, sing at your aunt's bunko night. Just sing! If you know you can do it for anyone, anywhere, anytime, you will have the confidence to nail it when it really counts— and you never know who's watching.

Now apply that to your dreams. If you are an aspiring Olympic pogo stick jumper—you ride that pogo stick every day for a set amount of time, rain or shine. Whether you're sick or whether you're cold or tired or hungry—you just ride that pogo stick! If you let excuses dictate whether you work toward your dream or not, you will sabotage your success.

Write down the top three dreams you have your life. If you're not sure, start with three things that make you happy, excited, relaxed, or motivated.

🖉 JOURNAL TIME

My Top Three Dreams:

1

2

3

3. FOCUS

"The harder you work, the luckier you get."

—ANONYMOUS

Have you read the great story about two expedition teams racing to get to the South Pole? One team was led by Roald Amundsen; the other, by Robert Falcon Scott. Amundsen's team decided that they were going to walk twenty miles a day—rain or shine—no matter what. Scott's team decided to only walk as far as they could, depending on the weather. Guess whose team won?

That's right—Amundsen and his team not only reached the South Pole first, but all returned alive. Unfortunately, Scott's team lost the race and also their lives. Every member of the team died, including Scott.

Jim Collins and Morgan T. Hansen coined the phrase "20-Mile March" in their book *Great by Choice*, where they applied Amundsen's goal of going twenty miles each day, no matter what, to the business world. This idea applies in everyday life just as well. Whether you want to start an exercise plan, learn a new language, or breed silk worms, setting a goal and consistently working each day to reach it is the best chance you have for success.

What is your 20-Mile March? What is the goal you are going to set and work toward every single day of your life? How hard are you willing to work to reach that goal? How badly do you really want it? Only you can decide, and only you can make it happen. If you don't have any dreams or ambitions, then don't worry about it. Sit back, relax, and eat some Cheetos while the rest of us put on our big girl pants and get to work. We are going to make this world rock! My guess is that you do have dreams and ambitions—otherwise you wouldn't waste your time reading a book like this.

One thing I have learned in the music business is that nobody, absolutely nobody, is going to hold my hand and carry me to success. I am the only one that really cares about my career and my dreams. I am the only one that wants it bad enough to make it happen, so it's all based on my work ethic and my efforts. If I want it, I am the only one that can get it. There are no shortcuts, and while someone may inspire you to greatness, you are the one who must do the work.

Some people certainly seem to have luck on their side. One of my favorite singers is Kelly Clarkson. Her win on *American Idol* seemed like she was an overnight success, but if you look at her story, you realize that she had been working and working for years. Because of her effort, when that opportunity came to be on *American Idol*, she was ready.

> *"Luck is what happens when preparation meets opportunity."*
>
> **—SENECA**

> *"Opportunity dances with those who are already on the dance floor."*
>
> **—H. JACKSON BROWN JR.**

Need any more cliché quotes, or do you get it?

Looking at the story of the South Pole expedition again, let me ask you a question. What was it that made Amundsen's team successful? I bet my boots that it was the fact that they set a firm, daily goal and worked hard, rain or shine, to reach that daily goal.

> "I may say that this is the greatest factor—the way in which the expedition is equipped—the way in which every

difficulty is foreseen, and precautions taken for meeting or avoiding it. Victory awaits him who has everything in order—luck, people call it. Defeat is certain for him who has neglected to take the necessary precautions in time; this is called bad luck." –*The South Pole*, by Roald Amundsen[1]

I want you to really think about what your 20-Mile March is. What are you willing to do every day to get what you want? I know I just said this, but—only you can decide, and only you can make it happen! There are no shortcuts.

Set a realistic, daily goal to work toward something very specific. Make that one thing your 20-Mile March.

Here is an example of a specific, daily goal: The dream is to become a professional hip-hop dancer. The 20-Mile March? Twenty minutes of uninterrupted freestyle dance time every day. You want your daily goal to be something that you will look forward to doing everyday but is also challenging.

One of the most important goals I suggest you reach for is to do well in school. I know it's hard, but it is so worth the effort! One thing that really helped me in school was to reward myself when I got my homework done. I couldn't watch my favorite TV show or bake myself my favorite dinner of deluxe mac and cheese until homework was done. That is a very worthwhile, daily goal that will make you feel like a rock star the day you get that scholarship or throw your graduation cap in the air.

So, if my goal is to get a 3.5 GPA this semester, I write that down. The next step is trickier. How do I do that? I write down three things that I can do every day to get there, perhaps: go to class (always helps), study one hour a day, and reward myself with my favorite Harry Potter movie when my homework is done. Your turn now.

✐ JOURNAL TIME

My 20-Mile March—write your very specific goal:

_____

_____

_____

_____

_____

What I am going to do every day to succeed in reaching this goal:

_____

_____

_____

_____

_____

_____

4. TIME MANAGEMENT SKILLS:

In order to be truly awesome with your dreams and goals, you have to learn the art of time-management.

BeingGirl.com gives us some awesome tips on how to effectively manage your valuable, limited time.

BE REALISTIC:

Like we talked about with your 20-Mile March—you must set a realistic goal or else it just won't happen, and then you'll just feel guilty. The whole point of going for our dreams is to be happy, so set yourself up for success!

> When looking to join an activity, be sure to understand the full commitment, including time and money. If you're able to make the commitment, go for it and have fun! Just be sure you allow enough time to study and complete your homework![2]

KEEP A CALENDAR:

Just being aware of daily, weekly, monthly happenings will ease your stress and help you stay motivated.

> A calendar is a great tool to help keep track of your homework assignments, tests, and school events. It's also a great place to add the following: your day-to-day activities, reminders for exams and projects, important events

like family get-togethers. There are a variety of calendars available, from pocket calendars to calendar apps on your phone. Choose what works best for you, and you'll soon find managing your time will become a habit. Another item to consider adding to your calendar is your period cycle. Tracking your period and understanding your cycle will help you be prepared. There are quite a few apps out there that make this so easy.[3]

PRIORITIZE YOUR RESPONSIBILITIES:

This is a hard one because there are so many things that just feel so important to us. This vital step in your time management will require some maturity on your part. Being mature enough to know that sleep is more important than watching that chick flick with your friends for the ninety-seventh time will be monumentally helpful to your long-term goals.

Learning to prioritize your responsibilities is important in managing your time. In addition to prioritizing schoolwork and family in your schedule, it is necessary to prioritize sleep. Sleep allows your body to function properly and helps with your ability to learn and concentrate. Prioritizing your responsibilities may mean reducing the time spent on your phone or computer, or even time with your friends. While your friends are also really important to you, you need to make sure that all your top priorities are being met before you schedule time with your BFFs![4]

TAKE TIME TO RELAX:

Remember our self-respect chapter? We know we can't be our best selves unless we take some time for self-care, and we certainly know that we can't reach our goals unless we take time to rest and rejuvenate.

> It's nice to be involved with everything, but you need time to just lie around and watch a movie or read a book. This is called relaxation. You need to relax every once in a while so you can revive your body and mind and prep yourself for a new day. But if you feel super stressed out, talk to your parents about how you are feeling. You can suggest that it'll be better to limit your activities because you are feeling overwhelmed. Be honest with them and they'll admire your maturity.[5]

When you manage your time well, I promise you will feel like you are on top of your world. It will ease your stress and help you feel in control of your universe. What could boost your confidence more?

RECAP:

1   **Identify your identity:** Understanding who you are and making decisions about who are will help you in every area of your life, but especially when it comes to making decisions about your future.

2 **Dream:** Let your imagination take you away! If you had no barriers, what would you do with your miraculous existence here? Allow yourself to dream up something truly magical!

3 **Focus:** Take that magical dream, and figure out a way to make it real.

4 **Manage your time:** No matter how talented, beautiful, or lucky you are, without solid time-management skills, you will set yourself up to fail. Don't let that happen. You were meant for greatness!

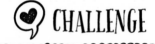

♥ CHALLENGE

Look at the dreams and goals you just journaled, and like Nike says, "Do IT!" Reaching your amazing goals all comes down to our—what? That's right . . . CHOICES!

WRITE ABOUT YOUR EXPERIENCE:

_____

_____

_____

GOAL-ORIENTED, CONFIDENT
WOMEN HAVE THE POWER TO
RECLAIM THE LOST ART OF
LADYHOOD AND CHANGE THE
WORLD!

CONCLUSION

I have one last thought to wrap all this up, and then I'll stop talking.

If you don't remember anything else from this book, I want you to remember my life philosophy. There's nothing really profound about it, but it has guided me in all of my decisions. It goes like this:

When I'm ninety and I'm sitting in the nursing home eating my pink Jell-O, playing bingo, and starring in the nursing home musical . . .

Will I be happy with the choices I made in my life?

It all comes down to our choices, and I want you to be able to look back on a long life of good ones. You don't want any regrets. You want to be able to say, "Man—that was a blast." So think about that every time you are faced with a decision. Take a minute and make up your own life-guiding question. No pink Jell-O required. ☺

✏ JOURNAL TIME

Just one last bit-o-writing fun—you know the drill.

MY LIFE-GUIDING QUESTION:

_____

_____

_____

_____

_____

_____

In life, we really only have three choices: to give up, to give in, or to give it all we've got. What will your choice be?

We need you, ladies. We need your leadership, your influence, your loveliness, your confidence, and your strength. You are unique and special. Celebrate what makes you extraordinary, as well as the things in your life that are extraordinarily ordinary— those are worth celebrating, too. You have gifts that can make a difference in someone's life. You have a beautiful purpose here. If you have a heartbeat, you have a purpose. It's your responsibility to do something with that purpose. I sincerely hope you choose to be confident—you are worth loving. You deserve all the happiness and success this world possibly has to offer.

If you use just one idea you read in this book, and it helps you—it has been worth the journey for me . . . and for you. I'm so excited for you to become everything you were meant to become!

I would love to get to know you and hear your story. You can email me directly, get some funky, free gifts, and find the link to all the meanings of my ridiculous "trucker talk" (Everything that 🚚 *LOOKS LIKE THIS*) at TheLostArtofLadyhood.com.

CELEBRATE WHO YOU ARE!
CHOOSE TO BE A CONFIDENT,
CLASSY LADY, AND ALWAYS
OBEY THE SPEED LIMIT. ☺

I sure adore you. Love, Jessie

TOOLS IN YOUR TOOLBOX

TOOL #1: FAKE IT TILL YOU MAKE IT (10)

Pull your shoulders back, smile, project yourself as confident, and no one will know the difference. This isn't actually faking it because this is truly YOU. This is the best version of yourself . . . a confident, happy leader. Own it!

TOOL #2: PEOPLE PLEASER CHECK-IN (16)

Pleasing is a dangerous game. Don't play it.

TOOL #3: GREAT WAYS TO SAY "NO" (18)

"No" is a complete sentence. Exercise your confidence by standing up for how you really feel.

TOOL #4: DRAGON WARRIOR (19)

We are the dragon warrior right now; we just need to choose to believe it. There is no secret ingredient.

TOOL #5: IDENTIFY SELF-DEFEATING BEHAVIORS (29)

Don't set yourself up to fail by sabotaging your own success. You were born to rock this place!

TOOL #6: LEADERSHIP HUNT (35)

Sometimes we have to learn and look for our leadership skills, but they are already inside us. Let them shine!

TOOL #7: GRATITUDE JOURNAL (47)

Focus on the positive things, and you will discover how many fantastical things exist in your life.

TOOL #8: SELF-DEFENSE AWESOMENESS (57)

You are worth protecting.

TOOL #9: SETTING PHYSICAL BOUNDARIES (64)

Decide right now where your boundaries are, and don't allow anyone to cross them. You are worth protecting. (Did I already say that? Yes, I did.)

TOOL #10: DINING WITH CONFIDENCE (73)

Having manners at the dinner table shows respect for yourself and others. It adds a little awesome-sauce to the food, too.

TOOL #11: SOCIAL ETIQUETTE ROCK STARS (78)

Simple acts of graciousness will go a long way when interacting with other humans.

TOOL #12: SERVE SOMEONE (98)

Step outside of yourself, and be kind to others. There are many unexpected benefits . . . increased happiness, stronger friendships, stronger family relationships, and more robust cuticles. (Okay, maybe your cuticles won't benefit, but your life will!)

TOOL #13: LOVE YOUR BODY (107)

Exercise and nutrition are essential for a happy life. Be kind to your miraculous, phenomenal body.

TOOL #14: RECORD YOUR MOM DREAMS (134)

Do you think motherhood is in your distant future? What do you want it to look like? Hide-and-seek, Disneyland, Christmas morning, running in the sprinklers . . . what kind of adventures can you dream up for your future bambinos?

TOOL #15: HAPPY ARSENAL (148)

The most valuable psychology tool I can give you. Drop-kick negative thoughts from your mind, and immediately replace them with happy, sappy ones.

TOOL #16: HOW SERIOUS IS IT? (156)

Step back and get a little perspective. Is it really worth the "ugly cry?" 😊

TOOL #17: THREE QUESTIONS (163)

Give yourself permission to believe that you are good enough. Are you as kind as you know how to be? Are you as good a friend as you know how to be? Are you as sincere as you know how to be? Well then, all is well! You don't need anyone else to validate your happiness.

TOOL #18: EMOTION PROCESSING—GET IT OUT (171)

Find constructive ways to channel strong feelings—hiking, ping-pong, crème brûlée, talking it out, journaling, playing your kazoo. Find what works for you.

TOOL #19: DON'T GIVE YOUR PERSONAL POWER AWAY (173)

Keep your power by standing up for yourself and being honest.

TOOL #20: THE C.L.A.W.—YOUR WEAPON OF DIFFUSION (180)

When dealing with bullies, stay CALM, LOVE them, AVOID them, and you will WIN!

TOOL #21: STRESS MANAGEMENT (184)

Stress is like "He-who-must-not-be-named" . . . oh whatever, let's just name him—Voldemort! It's an enemy. What is the best way for YOU to manage your stress and rejuvenate your mind and body? I don't know about you, but I have found the pogo stick to be incredibly relaxing . . . like a massage for asphalt.

TOOL #22: HYGIENE CHECKLIST (206)

When we take the time to put ourselves together, we are showing respect for ourselves and others. Everyone appreciates a lady who smells as clean as a freshly toasted strawberry poptart. (Wait, what?)

TOOL #23: THE POINT OF YOU . . . IDENTITY (220)

Who are you? Who do you want to be? What are your life goals? When you really know who you are, you can become the master of your universe!

FOR PARENTS' EYES ONLY!

First of all, thank you for buying this book for your daughter. I assume you bought it, that she actually read it, and has just now handed it to you since this says "For Parents Eyes Only." What an obedient daughter you have! I hope she has enjoyed the read and that she might have learned even one new thing that can help her life.

This chapter is for you—the parent or guardian of a teen girl. If you're anything like my parents, you are swimming in beautiful yet shark-infested water. Except that these sharks spend hours in the bathroom—primping and polishing, and they only take their skull candy ear phones out long enough for you to remind them to put on a jacket. Ten minutes ago these sharks were adorable, loving, cuddly, pig-tailed little princesses who wanted to hold your hand and have tea parties with you. You were their hero. They still have moments of being adorable and loving, but one wrong step can turn your princess into a foot-stomping, eye-rolling, jaw-snapping shark who screams, "You don't love me!"

You might be thinking, *This Jessie lady is mean—comparing my daughter to a shark.* You're right. I'm bold but honest—that's what I do. I'm only brave enough to call it out like that because I was the worst shark you can imagine. I think my behavior issues stemmed mainly from my lack of respect, both for myself and my parents. Why my parents didn't sell me to the gypsies when they had the chance—I'll never know.

I care so much about respect because some of my deepest regrets are how disrespectful I was to my parents, my teachers, my brothers, my friends, and basically any human around me! I wasn't taught how to respect people. My darling parents were going through so many personal challenges during my teen years that they were just trying to keep their heads above water. Living in survival mode can keep you from firing on all cylinders. I adore and respect my parents and have wonderful, healthy relationships with them now; however, even though they were emotionally, mentally, and financially taxed during my formative years, they still should have been tougher on me.

WE MUST TEACH OUR CHILDREN RESPECT

The truth is that when we don't teach our kids to be respectful, we actually handicap them. We set them up to have difficult relationships. We need to, instead, teach them how to handle their emotions in healthy ways. Kids need boundaries. Kids need rules. Kids need to be loved enough to have an authority figure tell them that their behavior is inappropriate and disrespectful. Our future mothers must learn the value of respect—for themselves and others.

Even though teens face challenges and live in a world where bad choices are popular, we don't have to coddle them. Here are five ways we can help our daughters by loving them enough to do hard things.

- Love your daughter enough to NOT make her life easy for her. She doesn't need to be saved every time she faces a challenge.

- Love your daughter enough to NOT put up with her disrespect. She does not need to be enabled.

- Love your daughter enough to NOT push her so hard in academics or extracurricular activities that you sacrifice the relationship.

- Love your daughter enough to NOT excuse bad behavior. Don't be in denial.

- Love your daughter enough to be authentic with her. Be willing to admit when you're wrong, say you're sorry, and ask for forgiveness. This is a great way to really connect with her.

 JOURNAL TIME

I gave your teen a bunch of opportunities for journaling throughout this book—it's only fair that you get a turn. Keep in mind, she will (hopefully) read your answers to these questions.

What are your top 5 favorite things about your teen?

_____

_____

_____

_____

_____

In what ways do you want your relationship to improve right now?

_____

_____

_____

_____

_____

What can you do to help accomplish that?

_____

_____

_____

_____

_____

What can she do to help accomplish that?

_____

_____

_____

_____

_____

What do you see for her future?

_____

_____

_____

_____

_____

_____

Describe her greatness.

_____

_____

_____

_____

_____

THREE C'S OF PARENTING SUCCESS:

CARING, COMMUNICATION, AND CHOOSING YOUR BATTLES

Caring: Don't ever give your daughter room to say "You don't care about me!" or "You don't love me!" Shower her with praise and love. Look for things to compliment, and look for really fun things to do together. They don't have to be expensive or elaborate, but put in some effort into finding creative things to do with her. Sharing your time will help her feel noticed, special, and listened to. There is no such thing as too much love. You don't ever have to put up with her drama, but don't ever give her room to say you don't care. Don't get me wrong here, she'll say it! But don't give her room to believe it!

The best way to show her how much you care about her is to give her your time. When she actually asks you if she can talk to you, drop everything and look her right in the eye and listen intently. When she seems down, ask her if she wants an ice cream cone at DQ with you. Ask her if she needs help with homework. Do puzzles or watch movies or play cards with her—find out what SHE wants to do when spending time with you.

I came across a great article from Focus on the Family in which the author, Joe White, was sharing his experience of raising teen daughters. He would go jogging with his daughter every morning at 6:15 am, but he had to follow her rules: "(1) We ran at her pace. (2) She did all the talking. (3) I did all the listening."[1]

Caring does not mean coddling. Caring means you are present, you listen, and you are engaged in her life. She has no doubt that you love her.

Communication: Create an environment where she WANTS to communicate with you! Get educated, and communicate with her about eating disorders, unrealistic expectations about beauty from the media, drug and alcohol abuse, bullying, cyber bullying, sex, sexting, teen pregnancy, girl drama, the importance of education, her long term goals, etc. You must become a master of the teen world your daughter lives in.

Our natural instincts make us want to give her a dose of reality, but you have to think back to when you were a teen and remember that "teen world" is everything when you are in it. To a teen, a friend's criticism is life shattering. If you roll your eyes at her and downplay the seriousness of her challenges, she won't talk to you . . . ever! She won't feel safe enough to talk to you. You must show her you care by being a nonjudgmental listener and by letting her feel her emotions—no matter how silly they seem to you. That is how you establish that she is safe. That is how you set the stage for great communication in your home.

Also be aware of your negative communication. Here's a story to illustrate:

When I was a photographer, one of my favorite annual sessions was with a junior high school dance company. Each girl was so lovely, but one girl really stood out to me. She was just stunning. I told her so during our portrait session and showed her my camera screen. She instantly scoffed and said, "Oh, I look hideous."

As the session wrapped up, I was on my way to my car just as all the parents were coming to pick up their girls. One lady was walking right toward me, and she had on an elegant, royal blue blouse. I told her I liked her shirt, to which she instantly replied, "Oh, I look hideous today." I watched her to see which young lady she would walk to. Sure enough, her daughter was the girl who didn't accept my compliment . . . just like her mother.

Our words have so much power—both moms' and dads' words. Our girls are listening, whether we know it or not. Try to be aware of your verbal and non-verbal communication. What are you subconsciously teaching your daughter about how she should view herself based on how you view yourself?

Lastly, communicate that you are not perfect. Admit when you are wrong, say you are sorry, and ask for forgiveness. This lets her know that you and she are in this life-thing together—just trying your best to figure it out. It will give her a sense of being on the same team as opposed to playing against each other. This is part of being authentic. When teens know we make mistakes too, they feel they can trust us and they are not so hard on themselves when they make a mistake. When I apologize to my kids, I add, "They didn't teach that at mom-school!" Kids need to know that being a parent is hard and that the stork didn't bring an instruction manual along with the baby. There is no reason to try to be perfect in your girl's eyes.

Choose Your Battles: Set yourself up for success by facing reality. Your daughter is going to say hurtful things to you, she's going to be snappy and disrespectful, she's going to make poor choices, she's going to distance herself from you, and she's not going to listen to your brilliant advice all the time. She is even going to flat-out disobey you. The sooner you accept that this kind of behavior simply goes hand in hand with teen years, the better and healthier your mental state will be.

I know it's hard to think about her having a messy room or forgetting to turn in an assignment at school or losing her wallet at the mall or even crashing her car in the school parking lot because her friends were distracting her. These kinds of things are hard to stomach, and it is sometimes hard to keep our cool, but these things are GOING to happen!

Remind yourself of when you were a teen—trying to figure out who you were, how to please your parents, how to remember all your homework assignments, how to keep up on your household chores, how to deal with the drama in your social circle—and all this amidst crazy hormones and body changes. Teens have so much to think about—they need to know you aren't going to freak out about every single, teensy, weensy mistake they make.

Yelling at her and taking away privileges every single time she makes mistakes will create a wedge in your relationship faster than the express line at Wal-Mart. Choose your battles.

ESTABLISH A "LINE OF RESPECT"

Rate the crisis on a scale from 1 to 10. If it's below a 7—LET IT GO. If you fight over little things, you might sacrifice your relationship with your precious girl. Don't do that—SHE NEEDS YOU! If she constantly feels like she's messing up and will never be good enough for you, she will eventually decide to just distance herself from you emotionally and fill the void with her friends. She needs you. Don't let her feel like she is a screw up.

Sit down with your daughter, and have a calm conversation about this scale. Establish TOGETHER what is and is not acceptable behavior in your home.

These are things I feel are below a 7 on the scale. Feel free to disagree—you decide what is right for your home. These are things that I consider annoying and hard, but in the long run, are less important than the 8s, 9s, or 10s.

BELOW A 7 ON THE LINE OF RESPECT

As much as possible ignore or let natural consequences take care of these:

- Being late for dinner because she is in her room listening to music: 2 on the scale.

- Messy room: 4 on the scale.

- Getting a B or a C on a test: 6 on the scale. If she gets a D, it's still not worth punishing or getting angry at her. Just ask her how you can help her, and maybe set a new daily rule that homework has to be done before she gets to hang out with friends or watch TV

- Being in an accidental fender bender (just have a long chat about making sure she isn't driving distracted. No phone use, putting on makeup, etc.): 7 on the scale.

ABOVE A 7 ON THE LINE OF RESPECT

These require immediate consequences:

- Eye rolls

- Back talk

- Yelling (at you or her siblings or even her friends)

- Tantrums of any kind

- Damaging things in your home—even in her room. Her room is still your property.

- Breaking curfew

- Lying

- Deliberately disobeying you or the house rules. (Each house hold has its own set of rules. Just make sure everyone knows the rule and the consequences—good and bad.)

- Any kind of law-breaking (obviously)—stealing, experimenting with drugs and alcohol, etc.

Decide where your Line of Respect is. When she crosses that line, a pre-determined consequence happens immediately. Respect should be a very clear line in the sand. Even something as small as an eye roll needs to be addressed. If you give a teen any room on this matter, she will think it is acceptable behavior. This cannot happen, because as soon as she thinks it is okay to roll her eyes at you, she will continue to push the line a little more by mouthing off to you. The next time she will mouth off in front of her friends to show how "in control" she is.

No matter where you have been in the past with your daughter, you can start fresh and establish this right now, today! Creating this Line of Respect has three beautiful benefits:

1 It makes your home more peaceful. No more yelling and no more tantrums.

2 It teaches her that YOU are the leader of your home, and that is the way it should be.

3 It teaches her that there are boundaries in life. You will be giving your daughter the beautiful gift of realizing that she has to exercise self-control when she is dealing with authority—teachers, bosses, future in-laws, and especially YOU! She has to learn that having respect for all

humans in our lives will not only benefit other people around her, but it will help her have a sense of positive connection to those people.

How do you accomplish all this? What does it actually look like?

First: Sit down with her when she is in a good mood, and have a very calm conversation with her. If she resists even sitting down with you, exercise your authority by threatening to take away something she loves that you can actually take away if you need to—grounding, taking her phone, not taking her to dance class that day (even if you lose money). The goal is to shock her into thinking, *Oh crap, maybe my mom/dad is serious this time.* Just get her to sit down with you so you can set your relationship up for success.

Second: Stay calm. She is going to TRY to get you worked up. She is going to try to push your buttons. Stay calm! Staying calm sends the message that you are in control—of yourself and your home. Remember, you are the leader of the house. You deserve respect from everyone under your roof.

Third: Always start a conversation with your daughter with love. Tell her how much you love her, how beautiful she is, how proud you are of things she's excelling on, etc. Make sure she knows that she is deeply loved and genuinely accepted by you. Then go right into introducing a new concept.

HERE IS A SAMPLE SCRIPT:

YOU: "So, I'm really excited! I have made an executive

decision for our home. It's called The Line of Respect. Have you ever experienced disrespect from any of your friends?"

DAUGHER: (Let her talk and really listen.)

YOU: "I hear you, I know exactly how that feels to get attitude and disrespect from friends. I hate that too. (Always try to relate to her without trying to be a teenager yourself). Let's write down everything you just said, and I want to write down a few forms of disrespect I don't like as well. (Notice, you don't even have to point the finger at her, just write everything down on a list. Your list might include eye rolling, yelling, tantrums, whining, complaining, snappy attitude, back talk, not obeying curfew, not following house rules, not listening, etc.) Do you think we have covered every aspect of disrespect?"

DAUGHTER: "Yep."

YOU: "Great! What is a fair consequence for crossing this Line of Respect?"

DAUGHTER: "I don't know . . . "

YOU: "Well, when one of your friends crosses your line of disrespect, what is a fair consequence for them?"

DAUGHTER: "I don't know, Mom. This is boring!"

YOU: (Breathe) "That's a bummer, but sometimes we have to do boring things. I just did the dishes this morning so I know how that feels. This is really important though, so I need five more minutes to talk about this with you. Let's say one of your friends gossiped about you behind your back and said some really disrespectful things. Do you think that kind of behavior needs a consequence, so it doesn't keep happening?"

DAUGHTER: "Sure."

YOU: "Well, any disrespectful behavior needs a consequence. As your mom it's my job to teach you that disrespectful behavior is unacceptable. So here we go. I think a fair consequence would be losing a privilege. If I cross your Line of Respect by yelling or snapping at you, I lose TV time at night for a week (or insert something you do purely for fun). If you cross my Line of Respect, you lose your phone for a week." (Or insert something that will really make her think before she rolls her eyes at you).

DAUGHTER: "A WEEK??? Are you freaking kidding me???" (This is where you breathe and stay really calm.)

YOU: "Okay, what do you think would be fair?"

DAUGHTER: "A day . . . maybe!"

YOU: "Let's compromise, if you cross the Line of Respect, you lose your phone for 3 days." (End of debate. You get the last say.)

DAUGHTER: "I HATE it!"

YOU: (Calmly but confidently) "I do, too. I hate disrespect. That's why this is so important. If we can just choose to respect each other, then there won't be a need for these consequences."

As soon as you post that list to your fridge, there will either be tension like you won't believe, or she will walk on egg shells for a few days. My guess is she will try to test you and see if you are really serious. Make sure her consequence is something you can absolutely carry out without question. If you are not consistent and dedicated to the plan—it won't work! Even if it is just a simple eye roll, calmly but firmly take the phone away for three days. She will pout and whine, and you just keep adding up the days she doesn't get that phone. It will be really hard at first, but as soon as she realizes you're serious and that you're not backing down, she will accept that this is a rule she must follow. Be tough. Don't back down, and always stay calm.

Keep telling her over and over again, "I love you too much to teach you that disrespect is acceptable." She won't like it, but she will get the message. Disrespect is unacceptable in the real world. It is our job as parents to make sure our kids learn that . . . even if it takes tough love.

Consistency is the key.

If you have a very defiant, tantrum-throwing, mean daughter, go to Skill #10: Personal Power. Look at the section about bullying and how you can diffuse it. I know it might be hard to hear that your daughter is bullying you, but we have to call it out in order to end it.

This book is based on the curriculum I developed and use for the National Non-Profit 501(c)(3) organization, The Ivy Girl Academy. I have gone through the 12 Skills of Ladyhood with your teen, and I want to share a few parenting tips that pertain to each of these levels. This will help you back up what I have taught, so real improvement and change can happen in their daily lives.

12 SKILLS OF LADYHOOD

1   **Confidence:** Help her find activities that she will rock! Give her opportunities to see and discover how talented

and awesome she is. Set her up for success. Confidence is the foundation for an awesome life!

2 **Leadership:** Help her find opportunities to lead. This doesn't necessarily mean she is the leader of a school club; it can simply mean she tries to set a positive example to others. Having said that, I strongly encourage you to help her explore entrepreneurship. This is such a great way to instill leadership qualities.

3 **Gratitude:** Take time to verbally proclaim how grateful you are for your life. Constantly look for things to point out in your world that you and she can be grateful for.

4 **Self-Defense:** Get her involved in a self-defense class. In my opinion, this is as important as learning how to brush your teeth or eat vegetables. This is a skill that will teach her so much more than how to defend her body. Look at the self-defense chapter for all the glorious benefits.

5 **Social & Dining Etiquette:** Etiquette is all about making those around you feel comfortable. You can start encouraging good manners today. The dinner table, cell-phones, her work, and social media are just a few of the areas in her life that she needs to learn how to be ladylike.

6 **Service:** Look for ways to serve others as a family. She might roll her eyes about it, but going to a soup kitchen, doing a food drive, going to visit sick kids in the

hospital, running in the race for the cure, etc., will plant priceless seeds of selflessness and fulfillment in your daughter.

7   **Health:** Help her set goals for exercise and nutrition. Go for a walk with her, take the time to prepare healthy meals in your home. The habits she creates at home will be carried with her for the rest of her life.

8   **Motherhood:** Talk openly about the benefits and hardships of being a mom. Also talk to her often about the importance of waiting to have sex until marriage. This will help her begin creating opinions of what kind of mother she wants to be and developing a healthy goal of waiting for the right time to get married and have children.

9   **Positive Mental Attitude:** Encourage positive self-talk. Maybe you could start a "love jar" where every time you or she chooses to say something positive instead of negative about yourselves, put a cotton ball in the jar. Once the jar is full you get to have a mom/daughter night out.

10   **Personal Power:** I know it is hard but we must have those hard conversations with our daughters. Drugs, sex, boys, respect—teaching her to face the hard things with open communication will empower her to feel capable of facing this challenging world.

11   **Self-Respect:** Teach her the importance of good hygiene, basic makeup, clean hair, and pressed clothes.

Even if she doesn't seem to listen, you are planting seeds that will grow when she is an adult. Good grooming is all about respect. If she takes the time to put herself together, she non-verbally communicates that she respects herself and others.

12   **Goal Setting:** Encourage her dreams—even if they are different than what you want for her. Listen intently when she talks about them. Let her try new things. Hopefully, she will have hard times and learn from those before she enters the "real world." Do not rescue or "protect" her from those valuable learning experiences.

SPECIFIC ASSIGNMENTS FOR MOMS AND DADS:

Dads: Talk to your daughter about how beautiful she is. If she doesn't get that kind of validation from you, she will go to the boys in her life for it, and that can be dangerous. Talk to her about how boys think. Tell her that what she wears affects the boys around her in ways that might make them uncomfortable. I know this is a hard conversation, but she needs to hear it from you!

Moms: Talk to her about puberty, periods, bras, tampons, sex, pregnancy, boys . . . basically everything that you know is going to get an "Eww, MOM!" reaction from your daughter. Talk to her anyway. She has to know it is safe to talk to you about these uncomfortable things.

HOMEWORK ASSIGNMENT

It is only fair that you get a little homework—your teen has to do it all the time. Write your teen a hand-written letter. Maybe you already do this regularly, but if you haven't written her a note in a while, this could really be special for both of you. Tell her how loved she is, tell her how proud you are of her, tell her all your hopes and dreams for her, tell her how badly you want her to be happy. From your heart, let her know she is precious and price-less to you. Leave it under her pillow, or put it in her backpack or somewhere she will find it and get a fun surprise.

I still have letters from my parents that meant a lot to me then and mean even more to me now. Think of it this way: it will never be lame to hear that your parents love you.

Letters like these are especially important to get from dads. Men are naturally less wordy than women, so getting a heart-felt letter from a father means so much. I have seen very positive results from this little activity. Your words have so much power.

RECOMMENDED READING

These fantastic books can help you further your understanding of your daughter and the universe she lives in. Education will be such a great tool for you as you navigate these teen years. Your girl is worth the investment of your time. I know you already know that.

- *Total Transformation* by James Lehman, www.TheTotalTransformation.com

- *Parenting With Love & Logic* by Foster Cline and Jim Fay, www.LoveandLogic.com
- *Queenbees and Wannabees* by Roselind Weisman, www.RosalindWeisman.com
- *Girls in Real Life Situations* by Julia Taylor
- *Think Confident, Be Confident for Teens* by Marci Fox
- *American Medical Association's Guide to becoming a Teen* by Amy B. Middleman
- *The Five Love Languages* by Gary Chapman
- *The Color Code* by Dr. Taylor Hartman

IN SUMMARY:

I know you love your daughter, or you wouldn't waste your time reading this. I imagine your daughter is a wonderful, sweet, darling girl whom you love spending time with. However, if your daughter is that wonderful, sweet, darling girl, but that goodness is buried beneath a layer of cynicism, surliness, and disrespect, then you have work to do. I am not saying her bad behavior is your fault, but you can help her! Education is the key! The books I recommended above are amazingly profound and effective. I also encourage you to really think about your Line of Respect. Giving your daughter boundaries can teach her so much more than just respect; they can improve your relationship with her (even if it gets worse before it gets better).

All in all, the most important thing is to shower her with love. Even when her bad attitude is so annoying you want to send her on a month long mission trip to Africa. Those are the times she needs the most love. Compliment her, look for the good, write her notes, surprise her with fun outings or gifts (which don't have to cost any money), listen to her without judgment, and be her parent—not her friend. She has plenty of friends; she needs a parent right now.

Your daughter deserves a consistent, boundary-abiding, loving, respectful home, and so do YOU. She is not the master of the house; you are. Making sure she knows that will be a valuable gift to her now, as well as when she becomes an adult.

I wish you the best in your journey through that treacherous yet adventurous world of teendom.

If you need or want any more help, I would love to connect with you and hear your story! I invite you to sign up on my website for monthly parenting tips. You can also ask me specific questions. Visit TheLostArtofLadyhood.com and shoot me an email.

"Successful parents are not the ones who have never struggled; they are the ones who never give up, despite the struggles."

—SHARON JAYNES

REFERENCES

CHAPTER ONE

1 Do Something.org. "11 Facts about Teens and Self-esteem." Dosomething.org. http://www.dosomething.org/tipsandtools/11-facts-about-teens-and-self-esteem (accessed August 1, 2014).

2 Kendrick, Carleton. "Building Up Your Daughters Confidence." Family Education.com. http://life.familyeducation.com/teen/stress/39305.html (accessed August 1, 2014).

CHAPTER TWO

1 Baskin, Steve. "Teaching Teens to Lead." Psychologytoday.com. December 6, 2012. http://www.psychologytoday.com/blog/smores-and-more/201212/teaching-teens-lead (accessed August 1, 2014).

2 David Letterman. "Jennifer Lawrence on David Letterman." Youtube.com, 12:16, March 20, 2012, https://www.youtube.com/watch?v=6GwpZS26MO8 (accessed August 1, 2014).

CHAPTER THREE

1 Tierney, John. "A Serving of Gratitude May Save the Day."

The New York Times, November21, 2011. http://www.nytimes.
com/2011/11/22/science/a-serving-of-gratitude-brings-healthy-
dividends.l?module=Search&mabReward=relbias%3Ar%2C%7
B%222%22%3A%22RI%3A12%22%7D&_r=0 (accessed August
4, 2014).

2 Emmons, Robert Ph.D. *Thanks; How Practicing Gratitude Can
Make You Happier.* Wilmington: Mariner Books. 2008.

CHAPTER FOUR

1 US Department of Justice. "Raising Awareness About
Sexual Abuse: Facts, Myths, and Statistics." NSOPW.
gov. http://www.nsopw.gov/en-US/Education/
FactsMythsStatistics?AspxAutoDetectCookieSupport=1
(accessed August 9, 2014).

2 Rape Treatment Center at Santa Monica UCLA Medical Center.
"Facts and Quotes." 911rape.org. http://www.911rape.org/facts-
quotes/statistics (accessed August 9, 2014).

3 Wharton, Sue. "Muscle Memory—It's All in the Mind." Journey
to Blackbelt and Beyond (blog), February 3, 2011, http://
kickasssuec.blogspot.com/2011/02/muscle-memory-its-all-in-
mind.html (accessed August 8, 2014).

4 Raleigh, Lisa. "Are Women Safer When They Learn Self-
Defense?" University of Oregon.edu. http://cascade.uoregon.
edu/spring2013/social-sciences/are-women-safer-when-they-
learn-self-defense/ (accessed August 4, 2014).

5 "Facts and Quotes." 911rape.org.

CHAPTER FIVE

1 "Etiquette." 2014. *Merriam-Webster.com.* http://www.merriam-
webster.com/dictionary/etiquette (accessed August 1, 2014).

2   Luddy, Joan. "Students Learn Respect Thanks to Good
    Manners." Educationworld.com. http://www.educationworld.
    com/a_curr/curr232.shtml (accessed August 8, 2014).

3   Cameron-Williams, Fiona. "Teen Etiquette—Table Manners
    & First Impressions." PR Newswire.com. http://www.
    ireachcontent.com/news-releases/teen-etiquette---table-
    manners--first-impressions-124034989.html (accessed August
    1, 2014).

4   Grotts, Lisa. "Five Questions with Etiquette Expert Lisa
    Grotts." *Seventeen.com*. http://www.seventeen.com/cosmogirl/
    lisa-grotts-mar10 (accessed August 4, 2014).

CHAPTER SIX

1   The Centre for Volunteering. "Alisha King—Selfless,
    Hardworking, and Dedicated." Youthvolunteeringnsw.org.

2   National Institute of Mental Health. "Depression in Children
    and Adolescents (Fact Sheet)." Nimh.nih.gov. http://www.
    nimh.nih.gov/health/publications/depression-in-children-and-
    adolescents/index.shtml (accessed July 14, 2014).

3   Smith, Melinda, Joanna Saisan, and Jeanne Segal. "Depression
    Symptoms & Warning Signs." Helpguide.org. http://www.
    helpguide.org/mental/depression_signs_types_diagnosis_
    treatment.htm (accessed July 15, 2014).

4   Smith, et al., "Depression Symptoms & Warning Signs."

5   Wenner, Melinda. "Study: Doing Good Makes You Feel Good."
    Livescience.com.

6   Wenner. "Study: Doing Good Makes You Feel Good."

7   Farino, Lisa. "Do Good, Feel Good." Healthyliving.msn.com.
    http://healthyliving.msn.com/diseases/depression/do-good-
    feel-good-1 (accessed July 14, 2014).

8   Farino. "Do Good Feel Good."

9   Farino."Do Good, Feel Good."

CHAPTER SEVEN

1   Williams, Allison, PhD. "Mental Health Benefits of Exercise for Adolescents." ACSM.org. http://www.acsm.org/access-public-information/articles/2011/10/04/mental-health-benefits-of-exercise-for-adolescents (accessed June 20, 2014).

2   Rufus, Anneli. "15 Shocking Exercise Facts." Thedailybeast.com. http://www.thedailybeast.com/articles/2011/08/19/exercise-tips-15-unusual-ways-to-improve-your-workout.html (accessed June 20, 2014).

3   Park, Madison. "10 Exercise Myths That Won't Go Away." CNNhealth.com. http://www.cnn.com/2011/HEALTH/06/24/exercise.myths.trainers/ (accessed June 20, 2014).

4   Daikler, Carl. *Insanity.* DVD. Directed by BeachBody.com. Santa Monica: Beach Body, 2012.

5   Levine, Susan. "10 Facts about Nutrition, Fitness, and Weight." Washingtonpost.com. http://www.washingtonpost.com/wp-dyn/content/article/2008/05/20/AR2008052001629.html (accessed June 20, 2014).

6   Coffman, Melodie. "How Many Teaspoons of Sugar Are There in a Can of Coke?" Livestrong.com. http://www.livestrong.com/article/283136-how-many-teaspoons-of-sugar-are-there-in-a-can-of-coke/ (accessed June 20, 2014).

7   Centers for Disease Control and Prevention. "Adolescent and School Health." CDC.gov. http://www.cdc.gov/healthyyouth/nutrition/facts.htm (accessed June 20, 2014).

8   "11 Facts about Healthy Living." DoSomething.org. https://www.dosomething.org/facts/11-facts-about-healthy-living (accessed June 20, 2014).

9 Langlois, Christine. "Teen Cooking Class: Help Your Teen Discover the Joys of Cooking." CanadianLiving.com. http://www.canadianliving.com/moms/food/teen_cooking_class_2.php (accessed June 20, 2014).

10 "Interesting and Fun Facts Fitness and Nutrition Facts." Crazyhealthfacts.com. http://crazyhealthfacts.com/interesting-fun-facts/fitness-and-nutrition/ (accessed June 20, 2014).

11 O'Sullivan, Therese. "Fact Buster: Does Eating Breakfast Help Kickstart Your Metabolism?" ABCHealthandWellbeing.net. http://www.abc.net.au/health/talkinghealth/factbuster/stories/2013/11/25/3898283.htm (accessed August 8, 2014).

12 "Interesting and Fun Facts Fitness and Nutrition Facts."

13 Zinczenko, David. "8 Ingredients You Never Want to See on Your Nutrition Label." Yahoohealth.com. http://health.yahoo.net/experts/eatthis/8-ingredients-you-never-want-see-nutrition-label (accessed June 20, 2014).

14 Healthy, Jim. "10 Ingredients We Should Avoid Like the Plague." Healthiertalk.com. http://www.healthiertalk.com/10-worst-food-ingredients-you-should-avoid-plague-4066 (accessed July 14, 2014).

15 Santanachote, Perry. "Banana-Oat Protein Smoothie." Dailyburn.com. http://dailyburn.com/life/recipes/banana-oat-protein-smoothie/ (accessed July 15, 2014).

CHAPTER EIGHT

1 Do Something. "11 Facts about Teen Pregnancy." Dosomething.org. https://www.dosomething.org/facts/11-facts-about-teen-pregnancy (accessed July 10, 2014).

2 Schuyler Center for Analysis and Advocacy. "Teenage Births: Outcomes for Young Parents and Their Children." Scanny.org. http://www.scaany.org/documents/teen_pregnancy_dec08.pdf (Accessed July 10, 2014).

3　Waiting Till Marriage. "Waiting Works: Couples Who Wait Report 22% Happier Marriages (and Better Sex!)." Waitingtillmarriage.org. http://waitingtillmarriage.org/study-couples-who-waited-have-happier-more-stable-marriages/ (accessed July 10, 2014).

4　Elliot Institute. "Abortion Risks: A List of Major Psychological Complications Related to Abortion." Afterabortion.org. http://afterabortion.org/2011/abortion-risks-a-list-of-major-psychological-complications-related-to-abortion/ (accessed July 10, 2014).

CHAPTER NINE

1　The Pursuit of Happiness. "Mindfulness and Positive Thinking Optimism." Pursuitofhappiness.org. http://www.pursuit-of-happiness.org/science-of-happiness/positive-thinking/#wrap (accessed July 11, 2014).

CHAPTER TEN

1　Koday, Dan, and Jodi Silberstein. "Real Girl's Guide To Dealing With Stress." Seventeen.com. http://www.seventeen.com/health/tips/stress-relief-tips?click=main_sr#slide-1 (accessed July 23, 2014).

2　Lowen, Linda. "10 Facts About Teen Dating Violence—Teen Dating Abuse Statistics." About.com. http://womensissues.about.com/od/datingandsex/a/TeenDatingAbuse.htm (accessed July 24, 2014).

3　Eccles, Jacquelynne, S. "The Development of Children Ages 6 to 14." Princeton.edu. http://www.princeton.edu/futureofchildren/publications/journals/article/index.xml?journalid=48&articleid=232&sectionid=1519 (accessed July 29, 2014).

4 Centers for Disease Control and Prevention. "Teen Dating Violence." cdc.gov. http://www.cdc.gov/violenceprevention/ intimatepartnerviolence/teen_dating_violence.html (accessed July 29, 2014).

CHAPTER ELEVEN

1 Raising Children Network. "Hygeine for Tennagers." Raisingchildren.net. http://raisingchildren.net.au/articles/ hygiene.html/context/1219 (accessed July 19, 2014).

CHAPTER TWELVE

1 Amundsen, Captain Roald. *The South Pole: An Account of the Norwegian Antarctic Expedition in the "Fram."* St. Petersburg: Red and Black Publishers, 2008.

2 Procter & Gamble. "4 Time Management Tips for Teens." Beinggirl.com. http://www.beinggirl.com/article/4-time-management-tips-for-teens/ (accessed July 23, 2014).

3 "4 Time Management Tips for Teens."

4 "4 Time Management Tips for Teens."

5 "4 Time Management Tips for Teens."

FOR PARENT'S EYES ONLY

1 White, Joe, Lissa Halls Johnson. "Tips for Parenting Teens." Focusonthefamily.com. http://www.focusonthefamily.com/ parenting/teens/tips-for-parenting-teens.aspx (accessed July 28, 2014).

ABOUT JESSIE

Jessie Funk holds a leadership certification from the University of Notre Dame, is a certified life-coach and is expected to graduate from Capella University in December of 2014 with a Bachelors Degree in Psychology, emphasizing in child and adolescent behavior. She has been hired to write national leadership curriculum for teen events and camps and she has been a keynote speaker for school assemblies and leadership conferences for teens for 12 years. Her passion to help teenagers led her to start a national non-profit organization called "The Ivy Girl Academy," a confidence and leadership-training program for teen ladies. Ivygirlacademy.com

As a professional vocalist she has released five solo albums, toured 36 states with the Broadway musical "Footloose," performed for former Vice-President Dick Cheney, opened for Donny Osmond, Josh Gracin and Billy Dean, Kenny Loggins, Collin Raye, and Belinda Carlisle, and toured with Broadway sensation Maureen McGovern. She has also been hired for hundreds of recording sessions as a studio vocalist including songs heard on TV's "America's Got Talent," ESPN, and "The Biggest Loser." Jessie's favorite role in life is that of adored wife and mother to two beautiful humans. To book Jessie to speak or sing at your event, visit jessiefunk.com.

ABOUT FAMILIUS

Welcome to a place where mothers are celebrated, not compared. Where heart is at the center of our families, and family at the center of our homes. Where boo boos are still kissed, cake beaters are still licked, and mistakes are still okay. Welcome to a place where books—and family—are beautiful. Familius: a book publisher dedicated to helping families be happy.

VISIT OUR WEBSITE: WWW.FAMILIUS.COM

Our website is a different kind of place. Get inspired, read articles, discover books, watch videos, connect with our family experts, download books and apps and audiobooks, and along the way, discover how values and happy family life go together.

JOIN OUR FAMILY

There are lots of ways to connect with us! Subscribe to our newsletters at www.familius.com to receive uplifting daily inspiration, essays from our Pater Familius, a free ebook every month, and the first word on special discounts and Familius news.

BECOME AN EXPERT

Familius authors and other established writers interested in helping families be happy are invited to join our family and contribute online content. If you have something important to say on the family, join our expert community by applying at: **www.familius.com/apply-to-become-a-familius-expert**

GET BULK DISCOUNTS

If you feel a few friends and family might benefit from what you've read, let us know and we'll be happy to provide you with quantity discounts. Simply email us at specialorders@familius.com.

Website: www.familius.com
Facebook: www.facebook.com/paterfamilius
Twitter: @familiustalk, @paterfamilius1
Pinterest: www.pinterest.com/familius

The most important work you ever do will be within the walls of your own home.